"A Link in the Great American Chain"

Studies in the Evolution
of the Orthodox Jewish
Community
in Cleveland, Ohio

Ira Robinson

TOURO UNIVERSITY PRESS

Library of Congress Cataloging-in-Publication Data

Names: Robinson, Ira, 1951- author.

Title: "A link in the great American chain" : studies in the evolution of the Orthodox Jewish community in Cleveland, Ohio / Ira Robinson.

Description: New York : Touro University Press, 2023. | Series: Touro university press | Includes bibliographical references and index.

Identifiers: LCCN 2023001244 (print) | LCCN 2023001245 (ebook) | ISBN 9798887191515 (hardback) | ISBN 9798887191522 (adobe pdf) | ISBN 9798887191539 (epub)

Subjects: LCSH: Orthodox Judaism--Ohio--Cleveland--History.

Classification: LCC BM225.C554 R63 2023 (print) | LCC BM225.C554 (ebook) | DDC 296.8/320977132--dc23/eng/20230119

LC record available at https://lccn.loc.gov/2023001244
LC ebook record available at https://lccn.loc.gov/2023001245

Touro University Press
Michael A. Shmidman and Simcha Fishbane, Editors
3 Times Square, Room 654,
New York, NY 10036
press@touro.edu

Book design by Kryon Publishing Services
Cover design by Ivan Grave
Cover art: Stained glass window from the Chibas Jerusalem synagogue.
Photo courtesy of the Maltz Museum

Academic Studies Press
1577 Beacon Street
Brookline, MA 02446, USA
press@academicstudiespress.com
www.academicstudiespress.com

To my wife, Sandra Moskovitz Robinson, who introduced me to the living community of Orthodox Jews in Cleveland, Ohio.

Enjoy happiness with a woman you love all the fleeting days of life that have been granted to you under the sun—all your fleeting days. For that alone is what you can get out of life and out of the means you acquire under the sun.

—Ecclesiastes 9:9

Contents

Introduction

This book brings together six articles I have published in recent years on the development of the Orthodox Jewish community in Cleveland, Ohio. The first of my publications relating to Orthodoxy in Cleveland dates to 2005. However, the beginning of my interest in this subject goes back nearly half a century. In 1973, as a first-year graduate student in Jewish history at Columbia University, I met Sandra Moskovitz, then a Barnard senior, at a Shabbat meal and we began dating. We married in 1976.

Almost from the beginning of our relationship, Sandy began introducing me to her family, and I began visiting Cleveland, Ohio, Sandy's hometown, on a regular basis. Starting with her nuclear family, and continuing with her extended family of aunts, uncles, and cousins, I began an introduction to the living world of Orthodox Jews in Cleveland. I prayed in Cleveland's Orthodox synagogues, particularly Young Israel of Cleveland, and frequented the community's bakeries, butcher shops, restaurants, schools, and other institutions.

Mi-kol melamdai hiskalti. In my frequent visits to Cleveland that often coincided with Jewish holidays, I began absorbing the atmosphere of Orthodox Jewish Cleveland, particularly from the perspective of Sandy's Holocaust-survivor parents, Margaret (Mindl) and Aaron Moskovitz, who spoke English well, but remained more comfortable in Yiddish, and thereby helped improve my grasp of a language that even in the late twentieth century was essential to fully understand what was going on in Cleveland's Orthodox community.

All these experiences prepared me in an important way for my intellectual interest in North American Orthodoxy, and the publication of scholarly articles and books relevant to the history of traditional Judaism in North America in general,[1] and in particular the history of the community of Yiddish-speaking immigrant Orthodox rabbis in Montreal,[2] that occupied me for a significant portion of my academic career. My developing scholarly interest in North

---

1   These articles are collected in my book *Translating a Tradition: Studies in American Jewish History* (Boston: Academic Studies Press, 2008).

2   *Rabbis and Their Community: Studies in the Immigrant Orthodox Rabbinate in Montreal, 1896–1930* (Calgary: University of Calgary Press, 2007). Cf. also my *A Kabbalist in Montreal* (New York: Touro University Press, 2021): *The Life and Times of Rabbi Yudel Rosenberg* (Boston: Academic Studies Press, 2021).

American Orthodox Judaism also prepared me to notice the publications of Samuel Rocker, editor of the *Yiddishe Velt* (*Jewish World* [JW]), Cleveland's Yiddish newspaper in the early twentieth century, which lay on a bookshelf in the Young Israel of Cleveland synagogue, and to take note of their significance for the history of North American Orthodox Judaism in that era. The encounter with Rocker's books at Young Israel laid the groundwork for my first publication in this area, which is included in chapter three of this book. Further thanks for that initial publication go to Steven Engler, a former graduate student at Concordia University, and now professor of religious studies at Mount Royal University. It was Engler who invited me to contribute an article on the subject of "historicizing 'tradition' in the study of religion" for a book he was editing, and I immediately thought of Rocker's books in that context. Engler's volume was published in 2005, and my contribution to it marked my first venture in the area of Cleveland Jewish communal history.

It would be another several years before my article on Samuel Rocker caused me to receive another invitation that would plunge me headlong into the global contemplation of Cleveland Jewish Orthodoxy and its development. Sean Martin, associate curator for Jewish history at the Western Reserve Historical Society in Cleveland, where he oversees the Cleveland Jewish Archives,[3] and professor of Jewish studies at Case Western Reserve University was in the process of organizing a scholarly conference that would reconsider the history of the Jewish community in Cleveland, and he wanted to make sure that Cleveland Jewish Orthodoxy was included. At the suggestion of my friend and colleague, Professor Jonathan Sarna of Brandeis University, who was aware of my interest in North American Orthodoxy, Martin asked me to contribute to his conference with a presentation on Cleveland's Orthodox community.

The research for my presentation at this conference, which involved extensive use of the rich resources of the Cleveland Jewish Archives, took place in the fall of 2014, and was greatly facilitated by my appointment as scholar in residence in the Laura and Alvin Siegal lifelong learning program of Case Western Reserve University in Cleveland. My thanks go to Professor Martin, Professor John Grabowski of Case Western Reserve University and the Western Reserve Historical Society, Professor Alanna Cooper of Case Western Reserve University, who facilitated my appointment as visiting scholar, to the helpful staff of the Western Reserve Historical Society, and last—and hardly least—to

---

3   "Cleveland Jewish Archives," Western Reserve Historical Society, accessed March 23, 2022, https://www.wrhs.org/research/library/significant-collections/jewish-american/.

my late brother-in-law, Eddy Moskovitz, and his wife, Iris, for generously hosting Sandy and me during this period. From the research I did at this time, I was able to write the articles that make up chapters one, two, and six of this book.

While my archival research in Cleveland was essential for the creation of this volume, it also impressed on me the knowledge that there existed much more material on my subject than I was able to access in the several weeks I had allotted for archival research on my presentation. It quickly became clear to me that any truly comprehensive work on Cleveland Orthodoxy would require a year or more devoted to research in the Cleveland Jewish Archives alone, let alone important material in private hands.

During my stay in Cleveland as scholar in residence, I became aware through a chance conversation while visiting a house of mourning of the existence of a private archive of the papers of early twentieth-century Cleveland Orthodox activist Abraham Abba Katz, now housed in a home in the suburb of Cleveland Heights. My research in that unique family archive yielded documents that formed the foundation of chapters four and five in this book. My thanks go to Abraham Katz's descendants, who welcomed me into their home and enabled me to mine the riches of the papers they had lovingly preserved.

While a number of scholars have ably presented important parts of the history of Jewish Orthodoxy in Cleveland, Ohio, this book is a first attempt to deal comprehensively with the story of Cleveland Orthodox Judaism. In presenting the results of my research, I am acutely mindful of the fact that, though Jeffrey Gurock has published an important social history of Orthodoxy in America,[4] a comprehensive historical account of Orthodoxy in Cleveland, or, indeed any major North American community has not yet been attempted.[5] I am mindful as well that the primary sources for such a truly comprehensive study, including many rich archival sources housed in the Cleveland Jewish Archives of the Western Reserve Historical Society Library, exist, ready to be exploited. Cleveland Jewish newspapers, including especially the Yiddish-language *Yiddishe Velt*, are also available to the researcher, and stand ready to provide important additional details for the history of Jewish Orthodoxy in

---

4   Jeffrey Gurock, *Orthodox Jews in America* (Bloomington: Indiana University Press, 2009).
5   Jeffrey Gurock has written a comprehensive history of Orthodox Judaism in a smaller American Jewish community in his *Orthodoxy in Charleston: Brith Sholom Beth Israel & American Jewish History* (Charleston: College of Charleston Library, 2004). Cf. also Ira Robinson, *Rabbis and Their Community: Studies in the Immigrant Orthodox Rabbinate in Montreal, 1896–1930* (Calgary: University of Calgary Press, 2007), which partially fills this gap for the Jewish community of Montreal in the early twentieth century.

Cleveland. This means that the chapters presented in this book are necessarily somewhat selective in nature and cannot truly do justice to this complex subject in its entirety.

On the other hand, in this book I feel like the archaeologist confronted with an extensive site, who does not have the resources to dig up the entire site. For that archaeologist, the exploration of a small, but well-considered portion of the entire site will yield useful details that can be extrapolated to create a depiction of the whole, pending the future excavation of further portions. In this spirit, I present the chapters of this book as a preliminary site report that will hopefully accomplish two things. Chapters one and two, taken together, will present for the first time a connected narrative history of the evolution of the Jewish Orthodox community in Cleveland, Ohio from its beginnings to the present. The succeeding chapters, for their part, will present in greater detail persons and institutions of great importance to the historical development of that community.

In chapter one, I attempt to sketch the evolution of Orthodox Jewry in Cleveland from its nineteenth-century beginnings to approximately 1940. This chapter will begin with a short discussion of the Judaic life of the earliest Jewish settlers in Cleveland prior to the coalescence of an "Orthodox" Judaism as a phenomenon of modernity that responded to the rise of a "Reform" Judaism in North America in the mid-nineteenth century. It will then examine the religious life of the Eastern European Jewish immigrant community from the late nineteenth century to roughly the beginning of World War II. Major issues dealt with in this chapter include synagogues, communal organizations, the rabbinate, Jewish education, and kashrut.

The account of the post-World War II period, in chapter two, highlights in particular the long-term significance of the establishment of the Telshe Yeshiva in Cleveland in 1941. It also deals with issues relating to Jewish education, synagogues, kashrut, and relations between the Orthodox community and non-Orthodox Jews. Finally, the article briefly surveys the state of the Orthodox Jewish community in Cleveland at the beginning of the twenty-first century with an emphasis on the impact of Orthodox educational institutions on the community.

Chapter three deals with Samuel Rocker, publisher of Cleveland's Yiddish-language newspaper, the *Yiddishe Velt*. It concentrates on the three books he published, all of which first appeared in the pages of his newspaper. These books include a volume on the Talmudic interpretation of the Bible as well as two books of Hasidic tales. These books show that Rocker served as a cultural mediator not simply between the Eastern European Jewish immigrants and their new country, but also between these immigrant Jews and their religious past, which included study of the Talmud as a highly valued religious and cultural activity, as well as the religious traditions embodied in the stories he told about the great masters of the Hasidic movement.

Chapter four examines one of the most prominent cases of "Orthodox" synagogues adopting mixed seating—that of the Jewish Center of Cleveland, which adopted mixed seating in 1925. However, a dissenting minority within the congregation refused to concede the principle that their synagogue, founded for the perpetuation of "Orthodox Judaism," had the right to do this. This ensuing legal battle attracted local, national, and international publicity and helped to define what Orthodox and Conservative Judaism in North America represented for an entire generation. This chapter utilizes archival sources not seen by previous researchers, which shed new light on the case and its consequences, particularly from the perspective of the dissident Orthodox minority.

Chapter five gives its attention to the story of the New Haven Yeshiva. The yeshiva was founded in New Haven, Connecticut in 1923, moved to Cleveland in 1929, and went out of existence in 1937. Likely because it had no institutional continuity in the postwar period, the existence of the New Haven Yeshiva has received relatively little scholarly attention. However, it merits our attention as the first Mussar yeshiva in the United States, patterned almost completely after the Slobodka Yeshiva. The New Haven Yeshiva's rise, as well as its demise, has much to tell us concerning the development of Orthodox Judaism in North America in general, and in Cleveland in particular, in the 1920s and 1930s.

Chapter six brings us to 1945, a pivotal year for Cleveland Jewry, which once again was preparing to move its institutions to a new neighborhood, Cleveland Heights. This chapter translates into English Rabbi Israel Porath's 1945 article on this subject, published in the *Yiddishe Velt*, that presented a remarkably clear analysis of the situation of Cleveland's Orthodox Jewry in that era, and a prescient vision of its suburban future.

It is my great pleasure to acknowledge permission to republish the material in this book that has been previously published, and to give the bibliographical details of the original publications, which make up this book. The material from chapter one previously appeared as "'A Link in the Great American Chain': the Evolution of Jewish Orthodoxy in Cleveland to 1940," in *Cleveland Jews and the Making of a Midwestern Community*, ed. Sean Martin and John J. Grabowski (New Brunswick: Rutgers University Press, 2020), 14–34. Chapter two appeared as "The Evolution of the Orthodox Jewish Community in Cleveland, Ohio, 1940 to the Present," *Studies in Judaism, Humanities, and the Social Sciences* 2, no. 2 (Spring 2019): 105–119. Chapter three was originally published as "Hasid and Maskil: The Hasidic Tales of an American Yiddish Journalist," in *Historicizing "Tradition" in the Study of Religion*, ed. Steven Engler and Gregory P. Grieve (Berlin and New York: Walter de Gruyter, 2005), 283–296, and was reprinted in my *Translating a Tradition: Studies in American Jewish History* (Boston: Academic Studies Press, 2008), 223–240. Chapter 4 appeared as "A 'Jewish Monkey Trial': the Cleveland Jewish Center and the Emerging Borderline between Orthodox and Conservative Judaism in 1920s North America," *American Jewish Archives Journal* 68, no. 2 (2016): 90–118.

Chapter five appeared as "The New Haven Yeshiva, 1923–1937: An Experiment in American Jewish Education," *Studies in Judaism, Humanities, and the Social Sciences Annual Review 2021-2022*, 333-351; and chapter six was published as "'The Second Destruction of Cleveland Orthodox Synagogues': Rabbi Israel Porath and Cleveland Jewry at the Crossroads, 1945," *The American Jewish Archives Journal* 71, no. 1 (2019): 46–56. These chapters were reedited for this book. Footnotes were standardized and, in some cases, new material was added.

My final thanks go to Professor Michael Shmidman, who heads Touro University Press, for his confidence in this volume, and to Professor Simcha Fishbane, also of Touro, for his collegiality and helpfulness over a period of decades.

Montreal, Canada
May 6, 2022

Abbreviations

AJYB: *American Jewish Year Book*
CJN: *Cleveland Jewish News*
ECH: *Encyclopedia of Cleveland History*
JTA: Jewish Telegraphic Agency
JW: *Yiddishe Velt / Jewish World* (Cleveland)
KFA: Katz Family Archives, Cleveland Heights, Ohio (photos of these documents are in possession of the author).
OJA: Orthodox Jewish Association
VKC: Vaad ha-Kashrut of Cleveland
WPA 1937: United States Work Projects Administration (Ohio), *Cleveland Foreign Language Newspaper Digest 1937*, vol. 3 (Cleveland, December 1939).
WPA 1938: United States Work Projects Administration (Ohio), *Cleveland Foreign Language Newspaper Digest 1938*, vol. 3 (Cleveland, June 1940).
WRHS: Western Reserve Historical Society Library
YABI: Yeshivat Adath Bnei Israel

CHAPTER 1

The Evolution of Jewish Orthodoxy in Cleveland to 1941

Nineteenth-Century Beginnings

The founders of the Jewish community in Cleveland[1] in the first half of the nineteenth century came to the shores of Lake Erie in Northeast Ohio with hardly any notion that Judaism could mean anything other than the traditional rabbinic Judaism that had existed in their ancestral village of Unsleben, Bavaria. However, they certainly understood that it was possible for Jews, especially in America, to be neglectful of the laws, customs, and mores of that Judaism.[2] Indeed, the "Unsleben document" of 1839 attempted to warn them of this possibility: "Do not turn away from the religion of our fathers. . . . Don't tear yourselves away from the laws in which your fathers and mothers searched for assurance and found it."[3]

When, in the 1840s, Jews in Cleveland began to create their own synagogues, they were designed to adhere as closely as possible to the only model of synagogue these Jews knew. Thus, Lloyd Gartner describes the first Cleveland synagogues in their beginnings somewhat anachronistically as "the two little

---

1   The major account of the history of the Cleveland Jewish community to the mid-twentieth century remains Lloyd Gartner, *History of the Jews of Cleveland* (Cleveland: Western Reserve Historical Society and the Jewish Theological Seminary of America, 1978). Cf. Sean Martin and John J. Grabowski, eds., *Cleveland Jews and the Making of a Midwestern Community* (New Brunswick: Rutgers University Press, 2020).

2   On American Judaism in the nineteenth century see Jonathan Sarna, *American Judaism* (New Haven: Yale University Press, 2004), 62–134.

3   Sally H. Wertheim and Alan D. Bennett, eds., *Remembering: Cleveland's Jewish Voices* (Kent: Kent State University Press, 2011), 196.

Orthodox congregations."[4] However, neither of these then traditional congregations, Anshe Chesed and Tifereth Israel, were "Orthodox" in the strict sense of the word, because "Orthodox" implies the presence of a religious alternative—"Reform" Judaism—which was then coalescing in Europe but which strongly manifested its intellectual and institutional presence in North America only in the mid-nineteenth century. It was in fact the leadership of Reform Judaism that designated those who resisted its claims to represent Judaism as "Orthodox."[5]

When Reform did make its appeal to American Jews as an alternative expression of Judaism that spoke cogently to their social and religious situation, Gartner notes that certain "Reform" tendencies appeared in Cleveland's synagogues (sooner in Tifereth Israel than Anshe Chesed). However, both remained essentially "Orthodox" for several years with Anshe Chesed housing a *mikveh* for ritual purification and both congregations employing *shoḥtim* (slaughterers) to ensure a supply of kosher meat.[6] Thus, in 1857, the anti-Reform traditionalist leader, Isaac Leeser, visited Cleveland and observed that "all communities in Cleveland are Orthodox . . . Reform does not seem to have made rapid progress. There are many who keep it [the Sabbath] holy."[7]

Cleveland's traditionalist community in the mid-nineteenth century included Joseph Levy, who had obtained traditional rabbinic ordination in Europe and settled in Cleveland with an extensive library of rabbinic literature but did not seek a rabbinical position. American Reform leader Isaac Mayer Wise, no friend of Orthodoxy, described Levy as "A learned rabbinical Jew of the oldest stamp . . . he stands firm upon the basis of the rabbinical literature, and commands respect from [sic] his religious position by his simple, firm, and decided language."[8]

In the 1850s Levy administered a Jewish divorce (*get*) in Cleveland that achieved a great deal of notoriety both locally and nationally. Part of the notoriety of this divorce likely stemmed from the fact that the divorce document was

---

4   Gartner, *History of the Jews of Cleveland*, 31.

5   On Orthodoxy as a product of Jewish modernity, see Jacob Katz, "Orthodoxy in Historical Perspective," in *Studies in Contemporary Jewry*, vol. 2, ed. Peter H. Medding (Bloomington: Institute of Contemporary Jewry, 1986), 3–17. Cf. Giti Bendheim, Menachem Butler, Jay M. Harris, and Uriel Katz, eds., *Jacob Katz on the Origins of Orthodoxy* (Cambridge, MA: Shikey Press, 2022). On the history of Reform Judaism see Michael Meyer, *Response to Modernity: A History of the Reform Movement in Judaism* (New York: Oxford University Press, 1988). For Meyer's account of early Reform in the United States, see especially ibid., 225–263.

6   Gartner, *History of the Jews of Cleveland*, 33–34, 38–39.

7   Ibid., 35.

8   Ibid., 38.

prepared and administered without the participation of Cleveland's only "official" rabbi, Isidore Kalisch. In any event, the *Plain Dealer* in Cleveland and the Jewish newspaper *The Asmonean* in New York opposed the Cleveland *get*, while Isaac Leeser's *Occident* not only supported Levy editorially,[9] but also published a learned responsum Levy wrote in Hebrew in which he defended the halakhic propriety of the *get* he had issued.[10] This constitutes the first published rabbinic responsum in the Hebrew language that was widely circulated in an American periodical.[11]

Orthodoxy and the Wave of Eastern European Migration to Cleveland

In the second half of the nineteenth century, Reform Judaism made important inroads in the Jewish community of Cleveland. Though the degree of liberation from the premodern Judaic tradition that was now defined as "Orthodoxy" varied from synagogue to synagogue and from family to family, two things are clear. The first is that by the end of the nineteenth century nearly all the mid-nineteenth-century German Jewish immigrants to Cleveland and their families had accommodated themselves in one way or another to the rhetoric and the teachings of American Reform Judaism, expressed both in German and, increasingly, in English. The second thing to note is that by the turn of the twentieth century the established German Jewish community in Cleveland had begun to note the increasing, and to them disturbing, presence of Jews stemming from the various countries of Eastern Europe who did not share their cultural, religious, and linguistic orientation. Though the individuals and families who made up the wave of Eastern European Jewish migration to North America in general, and to Cleveland in particular, varied greatly in terms of their geographic origins and their religious beliefs that ranged from militantly Orthodox to militantly atheist, the acculturated German-Jewish establishment of Cleveland Jewry tended to look at all the Eastern European Jewish immigrants, whom they

---

9   Ibid., 37.

10 *Occident* 10 (1852), accessed January 25, 2015, http://www.jewish-history.com/occident/volume10/jul1852/cleveland.html.

11 Personal communication from Dr. Zev Eleff, February 11, 2015. See Zev Eleff, "Power, Pulpits and Pews: Religious Authority and the Formation of American Judaism, 1816–1885" (PhD diss., Brandeis University, Waltham, May 2015), 91–93.

considered to be marginal to them both economically and religiously, as "Orthodox" regardless of their level of Judaic observance.[12] Thus, in 1895 Emma C. Davis broadly and negatively characterized these Jewish newcomers to Cleveland as: "These bigoted followers of the orthodox rabbinical law . . . whose minds are stunted, whose characters are warped and who have become adepts and who have grown wily in the evasions of law."[13] This mindset on the part of Cleveland's German-Jewish elite made for a situation in which the newly arrived Eastern European Jews felt it necessary to establish their own institutions, which included synagogues as well as a variety of self-help organizations.

Synagogues

The synagogues of the Eastern European immigrant "Orthodox" were characterized in a Cleveland newspaper article of 1887 as showing "the dark side of the European ghetto."[14] What do we know of them in the city that Rabbi Solomon Goldman characterized in the early twentieth century as "the most synagogue-minded city in the country"?[15]

I. J. Benjamin (1818–1864), in his account of his travels through the Jewish communities of North America, passed through Cleveland in January 1862. Beyond the well-established Anshe Chesed and Tifereth Israel congregations, he also noticed "a small Polish congregation, recently founded and as yet without a synagogue."[16] This congregation was undoubtedly Anshe Emeth,[17] which had been founded by Polish Jews in 1857. Other early congregations included Beth Israel Chevra Kadisha (Lithuanian, 1860)[18] and Bnai Jeshurun, founded by Hungarian Jews in 1866.[19] At the turn of the twentieth century, there were, in the words of a *Jewish Encyclopedia* article (1901), "no less than

---

12 Leon Wiesenfeld, *Jewish Life in Cleveland in the 1920s and 1930s: The Memoirs of a Jewish Journalist* (Cleveland: Jewish Voice Pictorial, n.d.), 61.

13 Cited in Gartner, *History of the Jews of Cleveland*, 110.

14 Ibid., 162.

15 Solomon Goldman, *Crisis and Decision* (New York and London: Harper and Brothers, 1938), 162.

16 I. J. Benjamin, *Three Years in America, 1859–1862* (Philadelphia: Jewish Publication Society, 1956), vol. 2, 281.

17 It is possible that the name of the congregation, Anshe Emeth (Men of Truth) is a dialectical comment on the name of the more established Anshe Chesed (Men of Lovingkindness).

18 Gartner, *History of the Jews of Cleveland*, 50.

19 Wertheim and Bennett, *Remembering: Cleveland's Jewish Voices*, 7.

eleven minor congregations, mostly Russian, with a combined membership of 700—the largest of them, Beth Hamidrash Hagodol Beth Israel, having 600 seat-holders."[20] The list of congregations in Cleveland in the *American Jewish Year Book* [AJYB] 1 (1899–1900) also lists eleven.[21] In 1923, Gartner states the number of Orthodox congregations to have been sixteen,[22] while seventeen Orthodox synagogues were listed in the 1935 Cleveland directory.[23]

The proliferation of Orthodox congregations in Cleveland followed several patterns common to most North American centers of Jewish population. First and foremost, congregations formed on the basis of European place of origin (for example, Lithuania or Hungary). Another criterion was the issue of liturgy.

Some congregations prayed in the Ashkenazic liturgy prevalent in much of Eastern Europe while others, like Nusach Ari, a congregation founded in 1906 that was apparently Hasidic, "a sect entirely new to Cleveland Judaism," prayed with the liturgy of Nusach Sfard or Nusach Ari.[24] Ultimately a Hasidic rabbi, *ha-rav ha-tsaddik* Meir Leifer became the rabbi of Anshe Marmorish Bnei Yaakov and founded a dynasty as the "Clevelander Rebbe" in Cleveland from 1922 to 1934 when he moved to Williamsburg, Brooklyn.[25]

Sabbath observance was another criterion. Whereas, for the most part, the Eastern European synagogues of Cleveland conducted themselves internally in completely traditional ways, many if not most of their members were no longer strict observers of the Jewish Sabbath because of the overwhelming economic reality of America, in which jobs enabling a person to observe the Jewish Sabbath and holidays were few and far between.[26] On the other hand,

---

20 *Jewish Encyclopedia*, s.v. "Cleveland," accessed February 10, 2015, http://www.jewishency-clopedia.com/articles/4420-cleveland.

21 "Directory of Local Organizations," AJYB 1 (1899–1900), accessed February 10, 2015, https://ajcarchives.org/AJC_DATA/Files/1899_1900_5_LocalOrgs.pdf.

22 Gartner, *History of the Jews of Cleveland*, 142.

23 Sidney Z. Vincent and Judah Rubenstein, *Merging Traditions—Jewish Life in Cleveland: A Contemporary Narrative, 1945–1975. A Pictorial Record, 1839–1975* (Cleveland: Western Reserve Historical Society and the Jewish Community Federation of Cleveland, 1978), 223.

24 Gartner, *History of the Jews of Cleveland*, 177. Cf. Ira Robinson, "Anshe Sfard: the Creation of the First Hasidic Congregations in North America," *American Jewish Archives* 57 (2005): 53–66.

25 JW, July 23, 1923, 2; JW, August 29, 1923, 2; "Cleveland (Hasidic Dynasty)," Wikipedia, accessed February 16, 2015, http://en.wikipedia.org/wiki/Cleveland_(Hasidic_dynasty).

26 One of the key issues facing motivated Orthodox Jews was finding work that did not involve working on the Sabbath. Organizations such as Cleveland's Jewish Sabbath Association were founded to help. Brudno's cigar factory, which was owned by an Orthodox Jew and which did not require work on Sabbaths and holidays, thus attracted, among others, "a few young men

some congregations wished to attract members who were strictly Sabbath-observant. Thus members of the Synagogue of the Government of Grodno pledged to strictly refrain from labor on Saturdays and Jewish holidays,[27] and the Hungarian congregation Shomre Shabbos, founded in 1905 on East Thirty-Seventh Street, only accepted Sabbath observers as members.[28]

Still another issue leading to the proliferation of synagogues was internal strife within congregations. Thus the issue of the separate seating of men and women, which came to largely define the difference between Orthodox and non-Orthodox congregations in the twentieth century,[29] arose in Bnai Jeshurun in 1904. The adoption of mixed seating by Bnai Jeshurun led to the founding of an Orthodox breakaway congregation, Ohab Zedek.[30] Anshe Emeth also debated this issue in the late 1880s. In this case, however, the dispute was essentially contained within the congregation until the point in the 1920s when, now united with Congregation Beth Tfiloh and transmogrified into the Jewish Center, the congregation opted for mixed seating in 1924 under the leadership of Rabbi Solomon Goldman amidst tremendous strife and great national publicity.[31]

In response to this momentous change in the Jewish center, Orthodox elements in the congregation led by Abraham A. Katz determined to fight what they regarded as a betrayal of Orthodox Judaism on the part of their

---

who were ordained rabbis and some 'genteel' young men who in the old country had never done a lick of work." These Orthodox men, "dignified, pious Jews with handsome beards," in Joseph Morgenstern's description, sat at one table and discussed Torah. This was a discussion in which Brudno, the owner, would "often" take part. Brudno is described by Rose Pastor as "a picturesque patriarch with his long black beard and his tall black skull-cap. . . . In this godless America he would give them plenty of work in a shop where the Sabbath was kept holy. It was his strength, for they would work in no shop where the Sabbath was not kept holy." Cf. AJYB 14 (1912–1913); Joseph Morgenstern, *I Have Considered My Days* (New York: Ykuf, 1964), 113–114; Wertheim and Bennett, *Remembering: Cleveland's Jewish Voices*, 87.

27 Gartner, *History of the Jews of Cleveland*, 133, 177.

28 "Shomre Shabbos," Jewish Cleveland, accessed February 17, 2015, http://jewishcleveland. weebly.com/shomre-shabbos.html (link not active now). The website of the congregation indicates the founding date of 1904: Shomre Shabbos, accessed October 14, 2022, https:// shomreshabbos.com/. Lloyd Gartner presents a founding date of 1906: *History of the Jews of Cleveland*, 177.

29 On this issue from an Orthodox perspective see Baruch Litwin, ed., *The Sanctity of the Synagogue* (New York: Spero Foundation, 1959).

30 Gartner, *History of the Jews of Cleveland*, 168–169.

31 Ibid., 171; Wiesenfeld, *Jewish Life in Cleveland*, 69–70. For an analysis of this incident in more detail, see chapter four of this book: "A 'Jewish Monkey Trial': The Cleveland Jewish Center and the Emerging Borderline between Orthodox and Conservative Judaism in 1920s North America."

congregation. They were initially advised by Rabbi Samuel Benjamin who had opposed mixed seating and had been recently ousted as the congregation's rabbi. They founded a short-lived newspaper as a rival to Samuel Rocker's Yiddish daily, the *Yiddishe Velt*,[32] whose main purpose was to fight Rabbi Goldman and the Jewish Center.[33] The conflict between the Orthodox group, which called itself the "Committee of 100" culminated in a suit against Rabbi Goldman and the congregation, alleging that the constitution of the congregation provided that as long as ten members will insist on the Orthodox ritual, the congregation had to remain Orthodox. The Jewish Center and Rabbi Goldman responded that the congregation's ritual and practice was fully in accordance with traditional Judaism. The issue in the trial became, therefore, what constitutes Orthodoxy.[34]

It is interesting to examine the Congregation's official response to the suit, for in its self-justification it illustrates the extent to which "Orthodox" congregations and individuals in Cleveland had been subject to "reform" influences:

> It is true that our congregation was founded sixty years ago, but for more than a quarter of a century it has been moving in the direction of what is generally known as Conservative Judaism.... Some twenty years ago we engaged as our spiritual leader the late Rabbi Samuel Margolis, who was known to shave, to eat without a hat, and seldom if ever attended daily services. Our congregation never pretended to be Orthodox. We have had late Friday evening service for more than a decade. We have had religious school and confirmation of boys and girls together for about fifteen years.... Ours was also one of the first congregations to join the United Synagogue of America. In 1921 prior to Rabbi Goldman's coming to our congregation we considered a merger with a well-known Conservative congregation in Cleveland.[35]

---

32 For more on Rocker and his newspaper, see chapter three of this book: "Hasid and Maskil: The Hasidic Tales of an American Yiddish Journalist."

33 Wiesenfeld, *Jewish Life in Cleveland*, 68. This attempt to found a rival newspaper was predictably heavily disparaged in the *Yiddishe Velt*. See JW, October 13, 1922, KFA.

34 "Testimony to Establish What is Orthodoxy will be Presented in Courts," JTA, November 4, 1927, accessed February 16, 2015, http://www.jta.org/1927/11/04/archive/testimony-to-establish-what-is-orthodoxy-will-be-presented-in-courts.

35 "Cleveland Center Leaders Reply to Orthodox Charges in Well-Known Controversy," JTA, November 20, 1927, accessed February 16, 2015, http://www.jta.org/1927/11/20/archive/cleveland-center-leaders-reply-to-orthodox-charges-in-well-known-controversy.

In the original trial in the Court of Common Pleas, which attracted national and worldwide attention, the judge ruled that the court had no jurisdiction over what amounted to a purely religious matter.[36] The Orthodox committee appealed the decision and initially seemed to have won when the Court of Appeals reversed the decision of the Common Pleas Court, and granted a temporary injunction for the Orthodox group against the Board of Trustees of the Jewish Center and Rabbi Goldman, enjoining them from using the synagogue as a Conservative house of worship, as well as a retrial. The decision was based on the plaintiff's contention that the synagogue was a trust, formed for Orthodox purposes, and that its trustees, without violating a trust, could not change the synagogue ritual from Orthodox to Conservative.[37]

However, the Orthodox victory was short-lived, because within a couple of months the Jewish Center leadership brought the issue before another Appellate Court, which concurred with the original court decision that the case centered on "a strictly ecclesiastical question" and again dismissed the suit.[38] The Committee of 100 appealed to the Supreme Court of Ohio, which, in December 1929, upheld the previous decision.[39]

The Jewish Center case ultimately served to more clearly demarcate the then often fuzzy line between "Orthodox" and "Conservative," and caused a great deal of bitterness between the sides. Rabbi Goldman in particular, who was the object of much of the resentment of the Orthodox side, seems to have reciprocated and harbored what Leon Wiesenfeld describes as a virulent hatred of the Orthodox whom "if he had the power, he would have exiled . . . to Siberia, as long as not to have them in Cleveland."[40]

---

36 "Cleveland Jewish Center Case Thrown Out of Court by Ruling of Judge Powell," JTA, January 18, 1928, accessed February 16, 2015, http://www.jta.org/1928/01/18/archive/cleveland-jewish-center-case-thrown-out-of-court-by-ruling-of-judge-powell.

37 "Changing Orthodox to Conservative Synagogue Trust Breach Court Rules," JTA, July 22, 1929, accessed February 16, 2015, http://www.jta.org/1929/07/22/archive/changing-orthodox-to-conservative-synagogue-trust-breach-court-rules.

38 "Court Dismisses Appeal on Cleveland Center Case," JTA, September 30, 1929, accessed February 16, 2015, http://www.jta.org/1929/09/30/archive/court-dismisses-appeal-on-cleveland-center-case.

39 "Appeal to Supreme Court in Jewish Center Dispute," JTA, November 17, 1929, accessed February 15, 2015, http://www.jta.org/1929/11/17/archive/appeal-to-supreme-court-in-jewish-centre-dispute; "Supreme Court Rules for Reform Wing in Cleveland Center," JTA, December 15, 1929, accessed February 16, 2015, http://www.jta.org/1929/12/15/archive/supreme-court-rules-for-reform-wing-in-cleveland-center.

40 Wiesenfeld, Jewish Life in Cleveland, 73–74.

Jewish Communal Organizations

By the early twentieth century, Eastern European "Orthodox" Jews had arrived in Cleveland in sufficient numbers and had acquired enough experience in their adopted land to realize that they had not achieved the recognition on the part of the established Jewish community to which they thought they were entitled. Thus in 1911 Rabbi N. H. Ebin and *Yiddishe Velt* editor Samuel Rocker demanded of the Council Educational Alliance that "the Orthodox element of the community" be more represented on the Board. Even though the Alliance responded by appointing Ebin, Rocker, and other representatives of the "Orthodox" to its Board, the issue did not rest.[41]

In 1923, the leaders of Cleveland's Jewish Federation commissioned a report by social worker Samuel A. Goldsmith (1893–1987) that surveyed the current situation of the Jewish community of Cleveland and pinpointed the discontent of the "Orthodox" as a major issue to be confronted by the Federation: "With the growing power and self-consciousness of the Orthodox Jewish group, every large Jewish community has had to face the difficult problem of unifying and coordinating the efforts of sometimes divergent views or interests within the Jewish community."

In this spirit, Goldsmith recommended that the Mount Sinai Hospital should provide kosher food for the patients despite the "personal customs or attitudes of the members of the board of trustees," that Federation should close on Sabbath and Jewish holidays, and that Federation assume responsibility for Jewish education.[42]

The recommendations of the Goldsmith report were certainly not implemented immediately to the satisfaction of the "Orthodox," as we see in the following report by the Jewish Telegraphic Agency in 1924:

> Cleveland has just now concluded its annual Community Chest drive for four million dollars and, just as has always been the case before, when the various sums allotted to each charitable and philanthropic organization of the city were announced our orthodox element found that they were not given their fair share. They are now complaining again that their institutions have been ignored and were not given anything even remotely

41 Gartner, *History of the Jews of Cleveland*, 225.
42 Gartner, *History of the Jews of Cleveland*, 284–285.

approaching what is due them in proportion to the substantial sums contributed to the Community Chest each year by the orthodox Jews.

Every organization of the Reform Jews in Cleveland receives a sufficient sum from the funds of the Community Chest to cover nearly all its expenses for the year. And in making the allotment the word of the reform institutions is considered sufficient as to how much they are entitled to. But it seems the orthodox Jews are considered step-children and are regarded with disfavor and suspicion.[43]

It was only in 1926 that Cleveland's Federation of Jewish Charities offered its first financial assistance to Orthodox Jewish institutions,[44] and during the financially lean times of the Great Depression the Federation refused to financially rescue Orthodox institutions, leaving an acute "mutual bitterness" that lasted for decades.[45]

In any event, the insensitivity of the established Cleveland Jewish community toward the specific needs of Orthodox Jews resulted in the establishment of several Jewish communal organizations designed to specifically serve an "Orthodox" clientele. Thus in 1906 an Orthodox Old Age Home opened its doors because the existing Montefiore Home for Aged and Infirm Israelites could not be persuaded to have a kosher kitchen.[46] Similarly an Orthodox Jewish Children's Home was chartered in May 1919 and opened in August 1920 as the Orthodox Jewish Orphan Asylum as an alternative to Cleveland's existing Jewish Orphan Home that was directed by a Reform rabbi and a predominantly German-Jewish board of trustees. The Orthodox home was established in order to raise the orphaned children in an "Orthodox Jewish spirit," and to place them with Orthodox families.[47]

---

43 "Our Daily News Letter," JTA, December 4, 1924, accessed January 26, 2015, http://www. jta.org/1924/12/04/archive/our-daily-news-letter-15.

44 Wertheim and Bennett, *Remembering: Cleveland's Jewish Voices*, 9.

45 Wiesenfeld, *Jewish Life in Cleveland*, 63.

46 In 1911 the Orthodox Home moved to 5912 Scoville Avenue (near East Fifty-Ninth Street), and in 1921 it moved to Lakeview Avenue where additional wings were built in 1929 and 1948. The institution moved to Beachwood in 1968 and changed its name to Menorah Park Center for the Jewish Elderly. "Union of Jewish Organizations," ECH, accessed February 12, 2015, http://ech.case.edu/cgi/article.pl?id=UOJO; Vincent and Rubenstein, *Merging Traditions*, 173; Wertheim and Bennett, *Remembering: Cleveland's Jewish Voices*, 9, 321.

47 Vincent and Rubenstein, *Merging Traditions*, 221; "Orthodox Jewish Children's Home," ECH, accessed January 26, 2015, http://ech.case.edu/cgi/article.pl?id=OJCH.

The Rabbinate

There were many Orthodox rabbis who came to Cleveland to serve the immigrant Orthodox community. They shared a commitment to the Talmudic culture and the Judaic law (*halakha*) in which they had been educated but were divided, as was the laity, by their geographic origins. Rabbis and other Jews hailing from Lithuania, for example, often did not get along with Jews of Hungarian origin, and vice versa.[48] They were also divided from each other because there were so few opportunities for Yiddish-speaking immigrant Orthodox rabbis to make a decent living. Many of the synagogues they served were not in a position to give their rabbi an adequate salary, and thus most of them depended, to a greater or lesser extent, on a position in the kosher meat industry of Cleveland, ideally as a rabbinical supervisor, or, failing that, in positions of lesser prestige and income, such as slaughterers (*shohtim*) and inspectors (*mashgihim*). The fact that there were never enough kashrut positions to give adequate work to all rabbis meant that the rabbis found themselves in a tight economic competition that constituted a major cause of the chaotic situation of kashrut in Cleveland until the 1940s.[49]

Despite these inherently divisive forces, the Eastern European Jewish community in Cleveland in the first decades of the twentieth century fostered several notable attempts to unite the Orthodox community and rabbinate. These attempts, however, could not withstand the powerful forces militating against such unity.

Leon Wiesenfeld speaks in his survey of Cleveland Jewish life in the early twentieth century of an unspecified "ludicrous attempt made by several Orthodox rabbis to elect in Cleveland a Chief Rabbi. The attempt ended in a fiasco and a scandal."[50] There are several such attempts to which Wiesenfeld might have referred. The first possibility happened in 1890 when an unnamed rabbi, reportedly from Pittsburgh, was elected chief rabbi of several Cleveland congregations but did not remain in the city for more than a few weeks.[51] A second possibility for Wiesenfeld's reference might have been the formation of an organization called the "Council of Cleveland Rabbis" reported in AJYB

---

48 Isaac H. Ever, *Rabbi J. H. Levenberg* [Yiddish] (Cleveland: Ivry Publishing, 1939), 520ff.

49 For an analysis of the entirely similar situation in the Jewish community of Montreal, Canada, in this era, see Ira Robinson, *Rabbis and Their Community: Studies in the Immigrant Orthodox Rabbinate in Montreal, 1896–1930* (Calgary: University of Calgary Press, 2007).

50 Wiesenfeld, *Jewish Life in Cleveland*, 124.

51 Gartner, *History of the Jews of Cleveland*, 174.

17 (1915–1916). A third possibility took place in 1918. In that year, twenty-four members of a "Union of Orthodox Congregations of Cleveland" voted to offer the chief rabbinate of Cleveland to Rabbi Maier Jung of London, who ultimately did not take up this offer, though his son, Rabbi Leo Jung did come to Cleveland to be the rabbi of Congregation Knesseth Israel in the years 1920–1922 and thus began his long and distinguished career in the American Orthodox rabbinate.[52]

A fourth possibility is Rabbi Benjamin Gittelsohn (1853–1932), who came to Cleveland in 1890 to be the rabbi of Beth Israel Beth Midrash ha-Gadol, which we have already seen was the largest Eastern European congregation in Cleveland in that era. An article in the *Yiddishe Velt* written at the time of his death in 1932 called him *zekan ha-rabbonim*.[53] This term signified that he was considered to be a senior rabbi, something of a *primus inter pares*. He was prominent enough to be featured among the profiles of American rabbis published in AJYB 5 (1903–1904).[54] Despite Rabbi Gittelsohn's prominence and his publications,[55] he was not able to strongly assert leadership over more than a few congregations.[56] Resistance to his leadership is evident in another newspaper article that appeared at the time of his death. That article remarked that Rabbi Gittelsohn's first years in the city, when, if ever, he would have tried to exert a leadership role, were not successful (*gliklekh*) because the congregations in Cleveland did not live in peace, his income (*parnose*) was not plentiful, and he therefore devoted himself to the study of Torah.[57]

An Orthodox rabbinical leader in Cleveland who never vied for the title of "chief rabbi," but whose career made a significant impact on the Cleveland Jewish community was Rabbi Samuel Margolies (1879–1917).[58] Margolies came to Cleveland with a unique preparation for the American Orthodox

---

52 Ibid., 178. On Rabbi Leo Jung, see Maxine Jacobson, *Modern Orthodoxy in American Judaism: The Era of Rabbi Leo Jung* (Boston: Academic Studies Press, 2016).

53 "Ha-Rav Gitelsohn 'enenu ki lakah oto 'elohim," JW, n.d., KFA.

54 "Biographical Sketches of Rabbis and Cantors Officiating in the United States," AJYB 5 (1903–1904): 58, accessed February 12, 2015, http://www.ajcarchives.org/AJC_DATA/ Files/1903_1904_3_SpecialArticles.pdf.

55 Gartner remarks that in his day Gittelsohn was Cleveland's sole productive rabbinic scholar (*History of the Jews of Cleveland*, 205).

56 These apparently included Ohave Emuna Anshe Russia, Shaarei Torah, and Agudath Achim. "Gittelsohn, Benjamin," ECH, accessed February 12, 2015, http://ech.case.edu/ech-cgi/ article.pl?id=GB1.

57 JW, January 3, 1932, KFA.

58 "Margolies, Samuel," ECH, accessed February 12, 2015, http://ech.case.edu/cgi/article. pl?id=MS9.

rabbinate. He was the son of one of the most prominent immigrant Orthodox rabbis in America, Moses Sebulun Margolis (Ramaz). His family sent him back to Eastern Europe for his yeshiva training at the Telz Yeshiva. When he returned to America, he entered Harvard College and graduated in 1902. He thus came to Cleveland in 1904 to become the rabbi of Anshe Emeth with the ability to preach and interact with his congregants in English as well as Yiddish. His rabbinical duties included encouraging the establishment of an Orthodox congregation in the then new Jewish neighborhood of Glenville, Beth Tfiloh, whose merger with the Anshe Emeth synagogue in 1916 gave rise to the formation of the Jewish Center on East 105th Street in the early 1920s. As the first English-speaking Orthodox spokesman in Cleveland,[59] Margolies took a leadership role in a number of short-lived initiatives to aid and unite the Eastern European immigrant community in Cleveland. These efforts included the Union of Jewish Organizations (1906–1909), which attempted to unite some forty-five community organizations,[60] a 1913 attempt to orga-nize a Cleveland Branch of the Union of Orthodox Jewish congregations of America that hoped to unite all local Orthodox communities,[61] and the Cleveland Kehilla (1913–1914).[62]

The Orthodox rabbi who over his decades-long career in Cleveland most approximated the role of "chief rabbi" was Rabbi Israel Porath (1886–1974).[63] In 1925 Rabbi Porath, who was then serving as rabbi in Plainfield, New Jersey, came to Cleveland for a convention and was offered a position by Congregation Ohab Zedek.[64] Beyond his rabbinic erudition, Rabbi Porath brought to Cleveland an ability to articulate his ideas in a nearly flawless English.[65] By 1927, Rabbi Porath was visibly taking a leading role in Cleveland's orthodox rabbinate and was well on his way to attaining the position of the representative Orthodox rabbi in Cleveland.[66]

---

59 Gartner, *History of the Jews of Cleveland,* 172.
60 "Union of Jewish Organizations," ECH, accessed February 12, 2015, http://ech.case.edu/cgi/article.pl?id=UOJO.
61 JW, July 25, 1913, 4.
62 "Kehillah," ECH, accessed February 15, 2015, http://ech.case.edu/cgi/article.pl?id=K2.
63 For a wealth of material on Rabbi Porath, see Yoel Porath, ed., *Mishkenotekha Yisrael: Hiddushei Torah, Igrot u-Ma'amarim be-Halakha va-Aggada* (Jerusalem: Porath Family, 2017). Cf. also "Rabbi Israel Porath, 1886–1974," Cleveland Jewish History, accessed February 15, 2015, http://www.clevelandjewishhistory.net/people/porath.htm.
64 Wertheim and Bennett, *Remembering: Cleveland's Jewish Voices,* 203.
65 Many of Porath's English-language sermons, including his inaugural sermon from 1925, are preserved in the Rabbi Israel Porath Papers WRHS MSS 4753, container 2, folder 7.
66 "Visiting Orthodox Rabbis of Three States Welcomed Here," *Jewish Independent* [Cleveland], July 29, 1927. Clipping in Rabbi Israel Porath Papers WRHS MSS 4753, folder 4.

However, Rabbi Porath did not fully achieve his leadership position at this point, because in 1929 members of the Cleveland Orthodox community attracted Rabbi Judah Levenberg (1884–1938), who was then serving as chief rabbi in New Haven, Connecticut, with the clear purpose of making him the primary Orthodox rabbi in Cleveland, and making his yeshiva, which he brought with him from New Haven, the nucleus of an experiment in establishing an institute of higher Talmudic learning in the United States.[67] Rabbi Levenberg's failed attempt to impose his rabbinic leadership on Cleveland Jewry, particularly with respect to kashrut, will be detailed below in the discussion of kashrut in Cleveland. The impact of Rabbi Levenberg's yeshiva will be discussed in the context of Orthodox Jewish education in Cleveland.

Jewish Education

The Eastern European Jewish immigrants in Cleveland sent their children to the Cleveland public school system. Insofar as Jewish parents desired Jewish education for their children, they would get that education, until the 1940s, entirely in institutions that were supplementary to public school education and in classes that perforce had to meet after school or on weekends. Rabbi Samuel Margolies expressed the nearly universal opinion of Cleveland Jewry when he stated, "we do not favor parochial schools."[68]

What, then, were the Jewish educational alternatives available? One was the Sunday school, which met once weekly. The Orthodox Sunday School movement in Cleveland was clearly inspired by the dominance of Reform Judaism in Cleveland,[69] a phenomenon noted by several Cleveland rabbis, including both Levenberg and Porath.[70] This Reform dominance was also apparent to the young people themselves. Cleveland Orthodox leader

---

67 On Levenberg, see Ever, *Rabbi J. H. Levenberg*; Moshe Sherman, "Levenberg, Judah," in *Orthodox Judaism in America: A Biographical Dictionary and Sourcebook* (Westport, CT: Greenwood Press, 1996), 131–133. For a more detailed presentation of Rabbi Levenberg's New Haven Yeshiva, see chapter five of this book: "The New Haven Yeshiva, 1923–1937: An Experiment in American Jewish Education."

68 Gartner, *History of the Jews of Cleveland*, 189.

69 Orthodox outsiders to the Cleveland Orthodox community noticed that Cleveland Orthodox rabbis would have a sort of "normal" relations with local Reform rabbis that did not happen elsewhere. Thus, in 1930 the Agudas ha-Rabbonim criticized Rabbi Levenberg for having published in JW a greeting to Reform Rabbi Abba Hillel Silver on the birth of his son. Ever, *Rabbi J. H. Levenberg*, 179–180.

70 Ibid., 306.

Abraham A. Katz recalls that, as a boy, he and his father "came together in a little Shul to pray and my friends attended temples decorated beautifully." He asked his father, "Why can't we have such beautiful temples to pray in."[71] At the Cleveland Jewish Center, while it was still officially Orthodox in the early 1920s, the congregation had adopted the ceremony of confirmation for its young people, a clear influence of Reform.[72] The example of Reform Judaism seemed almost irresistible and, as Rabbi Porath stated, to resist Reform "one had to fight against the current [of Reform] by going with the current."[73] Rabbi Porath described his own congregation's Sunday school, which was by far its most popular educational offering, in the following words:

> I must admit that I am not too much of an advocator [sic] of the Sunday School system. If parents think that they do their best by sending their little ones on Sunday only for two hours . . . they make a big mistake. If you want your children to become acquainted with Jewish religion, and be able to dawn [sic] and read, you must send them at the Hebrew daily.[74]

What Rabbi Porath meant by the "Hebrew daily" was an afternoon Hebrew school that met several times weekly and thus could present a broader curriculum. A number of these Hebrew schools existed in Cleveland, of which the most prominent organizationally was the Cleveland Hebrew School, often referred to also as "Talmud Torah." These schools, which trace their history in Cleveland to 1885, began in the early twentieth century to teach their students the Hebrew language in Hebrew ('ivrit be-'ivrit) to the exclusion of the traditional educational methodology of having the students translate sacred texts like the Pentateuch into Yiddish.[75] This innovation, as well as the perceived secular bent of Cleveland Hebrew Schools leaders like Abraham Hayyim Friedland (1892–1939), did not sit well with the more traditionalist segment

---

71 Abraham A. Katz, draft speech to the Union of Orthodox Jewish Congregations of America, 7, KFA.
72 The 1921 confirmation program is found in KFA.
73 Rabbi Israel Porath Papers, WRHS MSS 4753, folder 8. Rabbi Porath also presided over a confirmation ceremony in his congregation Oheb Zedek on May 9, 1937. Program preserved in KFA.
74 Rabbi Israel Porath Papers, WRHS MSS 4753, folder 7.
75 "Cleveland Hebrew School," ECH, accessed February 12, 2015, http://ech.case.edu/cgi/article.pl?id=CHS2.

of the community.[76] Thus, Rabbi Philip Rosenberg issued an undated two-page circular, likely in the 1920s, in which he advocated that Cleveland Jews not entrust their children's education to one, clearly referring to Friedland, who had recently given a public address praising the Jewish "apostate" Baruch Spinoza. Instead, Rabbi Rosenberg appealed to Jewish parents to send their children to the Yeshivath Adath Bnei Israel (YABI), a school more in line with traditional Judaic education as it had been known and practiced in Eastern Europe.[77] YABI, established in 1915, was characterized by Gartner as being "more or less a large ḥeder [traditional Jewish primary school] and provid[ing] bar mitzvah preparation."[78] It was certainly that, but another important factor was YABI's attention, at least in the higher grades, to the study of Talmud.

The study of Talmud had existed in Cleveland at least since the mid-nineteenth century and was actively pursued by adults in a number of synagogues, as can be seen in Rabbi Gittelsohn's first book, published in 1898, which consists largely of his speeches at the ceremonial ending of the study of Talmudic tractates.[79] Rabbi Porath, remembering the Cleveland Jewish community as it existed in the 1920s, recalled synagogue study halls "with Torah scholars [bnei Torah] who used to study daily classes [shi'urim] in Gemara, Mishna, Eyn Yaakov, etc."[80] The *Yiddishe Velt* in 1923 advertised a Talmud study group conducted, unusually, in Hebrew and led by Rev. Jacob Comet in the Ohel Jacob Synagogue at Scovill and East Fifty-Seventh Street.[81] That same year Ḥayyim Mikhl Frank, proprietor of a Hebrew book store, advertised, among other items, volumes of *Shas* [Talmud], *Mishna*, and *Ein Yaakov*.[82] But for the most part, Talmud study in Cleveland remained basically an adult activity, and, as Samuel Rocker remarked, most likely reflecting on his perception of the Cleveland community, one that attracted fewer and fewer men:

> [Here] we have abandoned it [Talmud study] completely and forgotten it. . . . Talmud study has become the possession of

---

76 On Friedland, see Sylvia F. Abrams and Lifsa Schachter, "Abraham Hayyim Friedland and The Context, Structures, and Content of Jewish Education," in *Cleveland Jews and the Making of a Midwestern Community*, ed. Sean Martin and John J. Grabowski (New Brunswick: Rutgers University Press, 2020), 58–79.

77 Undated circular, KFA.

78 Gartner, *History of the Jews of Cleveland*, 287.

79 Benjamin Gittelsohn, *Sefer ha-Poteaḥ veha-Ḥotem* (New York: A. H. Rosenberg, 1898), accessed February 13, 2015, http://www.hebrewbooks.org/2336.

80 Israel Porath, *"Der Tzveyter Ḥurbn fun Klivlander Orthodoksishe Shuln,"* JW, March 28, 1945, 2.

81 JW, July 27, 1923; JW, September 7, 1923, 11.

82 JW, August 26, 1923, 8.

a few individuals, while the people as a whole has no part in it. . . . [I]f this present situation will continue for the period of two or three generations, then, God forbid, the teaching of the Talmud will be forgotten among us, and even more so among our descendants in our country.[83]

There were some efforts to reverse this trend. In August 1923, the Cleveland Talmud Torah branch located at 2491 East Fifty-Fifth Street announced special classes in Talmud, which had hitherto been notable for its absence in the Cleveland Hebrew School curriculum.[84] However, it was YABI especially that tried to drum up the cause of Talmud study among Cleveland's Jewish youth. In October, 1923, for instance, a *Yiddishe Velt* report of a YABI celebration featured a recitation of the older boys who were studying Talmud (*di gemore kinder*). The reporter stated:

> The Talmud, that wondrous source of wisdom and science, has been here in Cleveland a closed book for our children. The Yeshiva [YABI] has demonstrated that also with American children one can learn *Gemara* and *Tosafot* with great understanding. It has also demonstrated to Cleveland Jews that the Yeshiva is the only spiritual center where Jewish children will be educated according to the correct traditional Orthodox spirit.[85]

But all these efforts put together did not seem to make much of a dent. In 1938, Rabbi Porath, who devoted his scholarly work over the course of a number of years to the publication of a multi-volume work entitled *Mavo ha-Talmud* (*Introduction to Talmud*), which attempts to make Talmud study easier both for young students who have never learned Gemara and for adults who had studied Talmud in their youth and had forgotten their learning,[86] and was in a position to know, could state that in all of Cleveland there were perhaps only twenty-five

83 Ira Robinson, "Hasid and Maskil: The Hasidic Tales of an American Yiddish Journalist," in *Historicizing "Tradition" in the Study of Religion*, ed. Steven Engler and Gregory P. Grieve (Berlin and New York: Walter de Gruyter, 2005), 286.
84 JW, August 12, 1923, 8.
85 "Yeshiva naies," JW, October 12, 1923, 7. Cf. JW, December 26, 1941, 2.
86 Israel Porath, *Mavo ha Talmud*, vol. 1: *Gittin* (St. Louis, 1942), introduction, unpaginated, accessed February 2, 2015, http://www.hebrewbooks.org/pdfpager.aspx?req=38100&st=&pgnum=2.

children who were studying Talmud and that in all the then-existing American yeshivot there were perhaps four students from Cleveland.[87]

A serious attempt to help rectify this situation in Cleveland was a project to establish a yeshiva, an advanced school of Talmudic learning, in the city. The project commenced in 1929 when Rabbi Judah Heshel Levenberg moved to Cleveland from New Haven with a mandate to bring with him the yeshiva he had founded in 1923, which was known as the Yeshiva of New Haven and which, in its Cleveland period, became known in Hebrew as the "New Haven Yeshiva in Cleveland" and in English variously as the "Orthodox Rabbinical Seminary of America" and the "Rabbinical Seminary and College of Talmud."[88] This Yeshiva existed until Rabbi Levenberg's death in 1938. Coming to Cleveland, Rabbi Levenberg had been promised by his Cleveland backers a salary of $5000 a year as well as an initial funding of $18,000 for his yeshiva, which then boasted forty students.[89] One of the reasons, perhaps, for his choice of Cleveland over New Haven was that the latter city was too close to New York, whereas for Cleveland, "there was no Torah establishment [mossad Torah] in it or in the nearby communities."[90] The experiment did not go well. Rabbi Levenberg's wife became seriously ill, and could not initially be moved to Cleveland. There was internal dissension among the yeshiva faculty.[91] Financially, the Depression hit the New Haven Yeshiva hard. By 1932 it was hurting for funds and appealing to the Jews of Cleveland for $5000 to keep its doors open.[92] At its end, Rabbi Levenberg's Yeshiva reportedly was down to only 14 students.[93] Levenberg's death was the factor that finally killed the yeshiva, and what undoubtedly helped to cause his premature death in his early fifties was his failed attempt to bring order to the kosher meat industry of Cleveland.

Kashrut in Cleveland

Kashrut in North America in the early decades of the twentieth century was an issue that seemed to lend itself to conflict. Harold Gastwirth's pioneering study

---

87   Israel Porath, "Vos hert zikh in dem Klivlander Ortodoksishn lebn?," JW, January 21, 1938, 5. Rabbi Israel Porath papers, WRHS MSS 4753, folder 8.
88   Yeshiva stationery extant in KFA.
89   Ever, Rabbi J. H. Levenberg, 159–160. Jewish Observer, n.d., KFA.
90   Ever, Rabbi J. H. Levenberg, 178.
91   Sherman, "Levenberg, Judah," 132.
92   JW, May 22, 1932, KFA.
93   Ever, Rabbi J. H. Levenberg, 330.

of the kosher meat industry in New York City at the beginning of the twentieth century bears the title "Fraud, Corruption and Holiness."[94] The title of the
chapter of Timothy D. Lytton's more recent book on the kashrut industry in
North America, *Kosher: Private Regulation in the Age of Industrial Food*,[95] entitles
the chapter dealing with this period, "Rivalry and Racketeering: The Failures of
Kosher Meat Supervision, 1850–1940."[96] There were important structural reasons for these "failures" that had to do, first of all, with the inherent conflicts of
interest between rabbinical supervisors of kashrut, the slaughterers and inspectors, the meatpackers, the wholesalers, the proprietors of kosher meat markets,
and the consumers. Most important from the perspective of this article, was
the non-hierarchical nature of the Orthodox rabbinate, which meant that each
rabbi could and did set up shop for himself with respect to kashrut supervision,
and would tend to resist with all his force anyone attempting to set himself up
as a "chief rabbi" with greater overall authority. This was a recipe for disaster.
And disaster came to the kosher meat industry in Cleveland in this period with
a vengeance.

Kashrut in Cleveland was an issue that, in the words of Rabbi Porath: ". . .
Embittered our communal life for decades and that constantly brought with it
so much desecration [*hillul ha-shem*] and distress [*agmat nefesh*] that it seemed
that kosher meat and conflict were like Siamese twins that cannot be separated."[97]
Isaac Ever, Rabbi Levenberg's son-in-law and biographer could only agree. He
expressed his opinion that never in the history of American Jewish life was the
problem of kashrut greater than in Cleveland.[98]

The fact that paying the costs of kosher certification made kosher meat
more expensive than non-kosher meat did not sit well with consumers at
the best of times. Thus in 1923 an advertisement of Cleveland's Warshaver
Kosher Sausage Manufacturing Company presented to the public the supervision team for its "strictly kosher" sausage: Rabbis Gittelsohn, Ozer Paley and
Zachariah Sachs and a permanent *mashgiah*, Rev. Jacob Comet. The point

---

94 Harold Gastwirth, *Fraud, Corruption, and Holiness: The Controversy over the Supervision
    of Jewish Dietary Practice in New York City, 1881–1940* (Port Washington, NY: Kennikat
    Press, 1974).
95 Timothy D. Lytton, *Kosher: Private Regulation in the Age of Industrial Food* (Cambridge, MA,
    Harvard University Press, 2013).
96 Lytton, *Kosher*, 9–34. Both Gastwirth and Lytton concentrate largely on New York. On the
    specific case of another major Jewish community outside New York, Montreal, see Robinson,
    Rabbis and Their Community.
97 "Vi azoi hot der merkaz ha-rabbonim bahandelt di kashrus frage letstn yor?," JW, October
    6–7, 1940. Rabbi Israel Porath papers, WRHS MSS 4753, folder 8.
98 Ever, *Rabbi J. H. Levenberg*, 211.

of the advertisement was a request to the public for its understanding that because of the costs of kashrut Warshaver kosher sausage's price was set two cents per pound higher than other brands.[99] However, from time to time the public's patience with this price differential wore thin, especially in a general social climate opposed to cartels and the fixing of prices, and the members of the Kosher Retail Butcher's Association of Cleveland[100] not infrequently felt the public's anger. Consumer discontent was given public expression in a 1906 strike against the high price of kosher meat.[101] Price was also apparently the main issue in a Cleveland kosher meat strike in 1928 that ended when Reform Rabbi Barnett R. Brickner of the Euclid Avenue Temple, acting as impartial chairman of a committee, brought about a reduction of two cents per pound in the price of kosher meat.[102] Discontent at the price of kosher meat in Cleveland would be a recurrent theme among Cleveland Jews to the end of the twentieth century and beyond.[103]

Beyond the issue of the price of kosher meat, there was the issue of the trustworthiness of kashrut. Was the expensive kosher meat the Jewish public in Cleveland was buying really kosher? The answer to that question was rarely an unequivocal yes. Public recriminations among kosher butchers, each of whom tended to disparage the kashrut of their competitors occurred often.[104] Similar public recriminations pitting rabbis against each other were likewise endemic. By the 1920s, the idea had spread among a number of Cleveland rabbis that the troubles of the kosher meat industry in the city might be solved by uniting the all the Orthodox rabbis into one organization, supported by an Orthodox lay leadership.[105] But which organization, and led by whom? In the mid-1920s one such attempt was the Cleveland Shechitah Board, which listed Benjamin Gittelsohn as its "chief rabbi," and Benjamin Botwin as its chairman.[106] Another attempt in the late 1920s was led by Rabbi Israel Porath, who presented himself as the "Chairman, Union of Orthodox Rabbis of Cleveland,

---

99 JW, July 23, 1923, 2.

100 AJYB (1907–1908): 358.

101 Lloyd Gartner, History of the Jews of Cleveland, 176.

102 "Lord Plumer Retires from Service on Half Pay," JTA, November 16, 1928, accessed January 26, 2015, http://www.jta.org/1928/11/16/archive/lord-plumer-retires-from-service-on-half-pay.

103 For example, "Kosher Prices here Found Neither Highest or Lowest," Cleveland Jewish News [CJN], October 31, 1975, 1.

104 Gartner, History of the Jews of Cleveland, 177.

105 For an entirely similar example of such an attempted solution of the kashrut issue in Montreal in the 1920s, see Robinson, Rabbis and Their Community, 87–102.

106 AJYB 26 (1924–1925): 539.

Ohio."[107] In describing the frustration he felt concerning the situation of kashrut in the city, as well as his vision of a way forward, Rabbi Porath stated:

> The orthodox rabbis of the city have worked indefatigable [sic] for the last four months . . . and it was all in vain, for the only reason, that Cleveland does not have a "Vaad haKhilloth" [Union of Orthodox Jewish Congregations] or an organized Kehilla, which will take over the business leadership of the arrangement.[108]

He further stated that "the voluntary [*freivillige*] work of the rabbis was not enough to solve the kashrut problem."[109] He foresaw that the answer to the problem might be strengthened Orthodox participation in the Cleveland Jewish Community Council.[110] Rabbi Porath's call for a solution to the kashrut problem was echoed in an editorial in the *Yiddishe Velt* of March 1, 1929, which charged that with respect to the issue of kashrut, Orthodoxy had failed Cleveland Jews.[111]

Rabbi Porath's plan was stymied by the reality that he was unable to get all Cleveland Orthodox rabbis to support his idea, and that he had no real authority to do more than engage in persuasion. To help in the process of persuasion, in August, 1929 a delegation of rabbis from outside Cleveland (one of several over the years) was called in to try to forge a compromise that the rabbis of Cleveland by themselves had been unable to achieve. One of the members of this delegation, Rabbi Judah Levenberg, who, as we have seen, was soon to move himself and his yeshiva from New Haven to Cleveland, described the kashrut situation in the city as one of "horrible [*shreklikher*] chaos."[112] As a result, in 1930 there was a conference of rabbis and lay leadership to found a body that would responsibly support kashrut in Cleveland, the Va'ad ha-Kashrut, fulfilling Rabbi Porath's vision.[113]

However neither Rabbi Porath nor Rabbi Levenberg, who had come to Cleveland in the meantime, were successful in coopting all Cleveland's

---

107 In AJYB 29 (1927–1928): 210, the group was called "The Orthodox United Rabbinate of Cleveland" and claimed to have eight members with Rabbi Porath as chairman.
108 "The Kosher Meat Problem of Cleveland," undated, Rabbi Israel Porath Papers, WRHS MSS 4753, folder 9.
109 Article in Yiddish, undated. Rabbi Israel Porath papers, WRHS MSS 4753, folder 8.
110 Article in Yiddish, undated, Rabbi Israel Porath papers, WRHS MSS 4753, folder 8.
111 Clipping in KFA.
112 Ever, *Rabbi J. H. Levenberg*, 158–159.
113 Ibid., 212ff.

Orthodox rabbis, and the forces opposed to the Va'ad ha-Kashrut brought what had been an internal communal feud to Cleveland's Court of Common Pleas.

In January, 1930 Judge Homer G. Powell ruled that the rabbis aligned with the Va'ad ha-Kashrut were not permitted to issue prohibitory decrees against slaughter houses not under their supervision. What led to this ruling was that a kosher meat wholesaler, Benjamin Cohen, who was connected with the Swift & Co. Meat Packing company, had refused to recognize the authority of the Va'ad. He determined to break its power by underselling kosher meat. In response to this move, the rabbis affiliated with the Va'ad ha-Kashrut proclaimed a ban on the slaughterers working at Swift & Co, alleging that the meat coming from that plant was not kosher. In response, another rabbi, Benjamin Botwin, who had been involved with Rabbi Gittelsohn on the Shechita Board in the 1920s declared that this ban of the Va'ad's rabbis was contrary to Jewish law. At this point, partisans of the Va'ad ha-Kashrut picketed the stores owned by Benjamin Cohen in which the allegedly non-kosher meat was being sold. This action sent Cohen to the Court of Common Pleas with a petition for a restraining order, charging that the Va'ad ha-Kashrut was engaged in racketeering through limiting the production of kosher meat and thus fixing prices.[114] Judge Powell's decision restrained the Va'ad ha-Kashrut from asserting either orally or in writing that the meat sold by Cohen on behalf of Swift & Co. was not kosher.[115]

Cohen then asked the court for a permanent injunction against the Va'ad rabbis opposing him. Testifying on his own behalf, Cohen claimed that his opponents were in cahoots with "gangsters to put him and his retail butchers not under supervision out of business." An attempt to bring about an understanding outside of court failed,[116] and when the trial resumed, Benjamin Botwin took the stand. Botwin was a former slaughterer and now served as the chief supervisor in the Swift plant. He declared in his testimony that whatever decisions the rabbis of the Va'ad ha-Kashrut had reached were contrary to Jewish law. On the basis of copious citations from rabbinic literature, Botwin tried to disprove

---

114 In New York City, the kosher meat industry was notorious for price-fixing schemes, racketeering, and even murder for hire. Lytton, *Kosher*, 3.

115 "Court Bars Rabbis from Passing on Unsupervised Kosher Slaughter Houses," JTA, January 30, 1930, accessed January 26, 2015, http://www.jta.org/1930/01/30/archive/court-bars-rabbis-from-passing-on-unsupervised-kosher-slaughter-houses.

116 "Kosher Meat Controversy Stirs Jews of Cleveland and Neighboring Towns," JTA, February 14, 1930, accessed January 26, 2015, http://www.jta.org/1930/02/14/archive/kosher-meat-controversy-stirs-jews-of-cleveland-and-neighboring-towns.

the claim that rabbis could ban a slaughterer or that supervision over slaughter-houses and butcher shops was required.[117]

In the end, the extensive publicity given the case both in Cleveland and throughout the Jewish world[118] caused the management of Swift & Co. to attempt to stop the proceedings and work out a compromise agreement to be supervised by a rabbinical reconciliation committee of five composed of two local rabbis, two out-of-town rabbis and one rabbi from the Union of Orthodox Rabbis (Agudas ha-Rabbonim).[119] In the out of court settlement, Swift agreed to give the Va'ad ha-Kashrut and its rabbis full recognition. However, Cohen remained opposed to the agreement, and declared he would not recognize the rabbis and the Va'ad ha-Kashrut. Thus, the issue continued to divide the Cleveland rabbinate and Jewish community.[120]

In 1932, these underlying tensions broke out again when Rabbi Judah Levenberg once again attempted to unite the Orthodox rabbinate of Cleveland and its lay leadership and solve the problem of kashrut under his leadership. This attempt embraced almost all the Orthodox rabbis in Cleveland, but pre-dictably not all of them.[121] Levenberg's organization, called the Federation of Orthodox Jewish Congregations (Va'ad ha-Kehillot), claimed to represent twenty-one orthodox congregations in Cleveland with nearly 15,000 members.

As a possible way out of the impasse that had stymied previous efforts, the Va'ad ha-Kehillot proposed to have its rabbinic leadership (*bet din*) elected by popular vote of the city's Orthodox Jews in the hope that this would give it the popular mandate required to regulate the kashrut industry. This unusual move was possibly inspired by the fact that, in the State of Ohio, all judges are popu-larly elected.[122] In this election over 3000 voters, who included women as well as men, gave Rabbi Levenberg the preponderance of votes (1770 as opposed

---

117 "Cleveland Kashruth Case May End in Few Days," JTA, February 21, 1930, accessed January 26, 2015, http://www.jta.org/1930/02/21/archive/cleveland-kashruth-case-may-end-in-few-days.

118 A writer in Montreal's Yiddish daily *Keneder 'Adler*, February 20, 1930, 1, said that he next expected that the witness would produce testimony against his rabbinical opponents from the *Protocols of the Elders of Zion*.

119 "Cleveland Kashruth Case May Be Settled by Arbitration," JTA, February 24, 1930, accessed January 26, 2015, http://www.jta.org/1930/02/24/archive/cleveland-kashruth-case-may-be-settled-by-arbitration.

120 "Settlement in Cleveland's Kashruth Case Favorable to Jews Laid to J. T. A.," JTA, February 26, 1930, accessed January 26, 2015, http://www.jta.org/1930/02/26/archive/settlement-in-clevelands-kashruth-case-favorable-to-jews-laid-to-j-t-a-2.

121 Ever, *Rabbi J. H. Levenberg*, 204–207, 215–216.

122 "Article IV, Ohio Constitution," accessed February 9, 2015, http://judgepedia.org/Article_IV,_Ohio_Constitution.

to 689 for his nearest rival, Rabbi Krislov),[123] though his opponents charged that the vote was fraudulent and that Rabbi Levenberg's partisans had even brought in non-Jews to vote for him.[124]

In December 1932 Levenberg's new organization called for the investigation of all the kosher butcher shops in Cleveland for alleged "racketeering" in meat prices as well as other irregularities in butcher shops and poultry markets. It also hoped, in partnership with City of Cleveland food inspectors, to regulate sanitation, stabilize prices and eliminate fraud in the kosher trade by creating kosher market licenses to be issued by the city of Cleveland and supervised by a committee of rabbis to be appointed by the mayor. A first step in this direction would be an investigation by the Cuyahoga county prosecutor's office of a newly established Independent Kosher Meat Association.[125]

This threat unleashed "a wave of racketeering and crime" involving kosher butcher shops in Cleveland, which included broken shop windows and stench bombs. This wave was climaxed by two incidents in which a Jewish poultry market owned by William Danches was bombed, possibly because Danches's shop charged only five cents for the kosher slaughter of chickens, thereby undercutting the standard rate of ten cents. The second time, the explosion reportedly "ripped a hole in the wall of the poultry market and tore down the roof." Danches told police that he had recently refused to pay 2 cents on each chicken killed at his market to a "racket organization." By this, he meant the Federation of Orthodox Jewish Congregations, which demanded that there be a two-cent charge on each chicken slaughtered to help defray its supervision expenses, a demand that was resisted by many poultry slaughterers.[126]

On the basis of the testimony of Mr. and Mrs. Danches, and Yeshaiah Bauer, a poultry slaughterer,[127] police warrants were issued by the Cuyahoga

---

123 Ever, *Rabbi J. H. Levenberg*, 292. Cf. undated JW clipping in Abraham A. Katz Archives, Cleveland Heights, Ohio.

124 Ever, *Rabbi J. H. Levenberg*, 299.

125 "Cleveland Kosher Butcher Shops to Be Investigated for Alleged 'Racketeering,'" JTA, December 29, 1932, accessed January 26, 2015, http://www.jta.org/1932/12/29/archive/cleveland-kosher-butcher-shops-to-be-investigated-for-alleged-racketeering. This move may have been inspired by the 1931 report of the New York City Mayor's Committee on Kashrut that recommended the establishment of an organization consisting of rabbis from throughout the city and lay representatives with a charter from the state to exercise "quasi-public powers in matters pertaining to kashruth supervision," as a result of which, with encouragement from the mayor, members of the committee established the Kashruth Association of Greater New York in 1932 "to aid in and encourage the observance and enforcement" of the Kosher Law. Lytton, *Kosher*, 29.

126 Circular of protest by the poultry slaughterers against the two-cent levy. Found in KFA.

127 Ever, *Rabbi J. H. Levenberg*, 221–242.

County Prosecutor's office for three men, accused by Danches of having threatened him.[128] The result of these accusations was the arrest of Rabbi Levenberg at 3:00 a.m. on a Friday morning. He was held in police custody all day before he was released. The next Sunday, the rabbi's arrest was protested in a mass meeting attended by an estimated 2,500 people and resulted in an apology from Cleveland's Director of Public Safety, Frank J. Merrick, and a dismissal of the charges against Rabbi Levenberg.[129]

That did not mark the end of Rabbi Levenberg's troubles, however. In early April, 1933, a brick was thrown through the window of Levenberg's home. As the Jewish Telegraphic Agency report stated: "The brick was wrapped in a circular on one side of which was printed: 'This is only a warning. Steps will follow.' On the other side was written a protest against the discharge of Herman Weisberger, a schochet, from the American Poultry market."[130]

In the meantime, the rabbinic opposition to Rabbi Levenberg, led by Rabbi Phillip Rosenberg, organized a rival Misrad ha-Rabbonim of Cleveland, which became a continuing thorn in the side of Rabbi Levenberg and his partisans.[131] The Misrad, which reportedly included Rabbis Rosenberg, Berger, Eckstein, Shapiro, and Schwartz, was in a fairly strong position because it maintained financially viable contracts with slaughterhouses like Swift & Company,[132] and so did not feel the need to compromise.[133] Those rabbis, like Porath, Paley, and Krislov, who continued to try talking to both sides, became suspect.[134]

With the rabbis fighting among themselves, the sixty-four members of the Independent Kosher Butchers Association did not know which rabbis to obey and resolved not to let any outside kashrut supervisors (*mashgihim*) into their shops.[135] On September 4, 1933, a *Yiddishe Velt* editorial spoke of a Cleveland kashrut that was lawless (*hefker*) despite the efforts of the Union

---

128 "Cleveland Jewish Poultry Market Bombed in 'Racketeering War,'" JTA, January 22, 1933, accessed January 26, 2015, http://www.jta.org/1933/01/22/archive/cleveland-jewish-poultry-market-bombed-in-racketeering-war.

129 "'Racketeering War' Leads to Arrest of Yeshiva Dean; Police Apologize; Dismiss Charges," JTA, January 26, 1933, accessed January 26, 2015, http://www.jta.org/1933/01/26/archive/racketeering-war-leads-to-arrest-of-yeshiva-dean-police-apologize-dismiss-charges.

130 "Life of North American Jewry in Review," JTA, April 3, 1934, accessed January 26, 2015, http://www.jta.org/1934/04/03/archive/life-of-north-american-jewry-in-review-36.

131 Ever, *Rabbi J. H. Levenberg*, 247–248.

132 JW editorial, November 16, 1934, 4.

133 Ever, *Rabbi J. H. Levenberg*, 279–281; cf. JW editorial, October 25, 1934.

134 Ever, *Rabbi J. H. Levenberg*, 282, 285–288.

135 Advertisement in JW, October 19, 1934, 8; JW, November 18, 1934, 8.

of the twenty-nine Orthodox congregations to create order out of chaos. The newspaper looked forward to yet another delegation of outside rabbis, this one led by Cincinnati's Rabbi Eliezer Silver.[136] In a further editorial, in 1934, the *Yiddishe Velt* stated that while there was never a time that disputes over kosher meat did not exist, this level of dissension had not been witnessed either in Cleveland or in any other Jewish community in America.[137]

The chaotic situation apparently lasted for several years so that in 1940, Rabbi Porath, who had returned to a leadership position among Cleveland's Orthodox rabbis after Rabbi Levenberg's death, reported that Cleveland Jewry had lived for many years without any supervision (*hashgaha*) in kosher meat markets. He described a situation in which the "truly kosher" butchers were unable to meet their competitors in price, and consumers were never completely certain that the meat they were buying was truly kosher. He further reported that there was not one restaurant in Cleveland that could be considered reliably kosher.[138] This situation is starkly depicted in the report of the Committee of Kashruth of the Jewish Community Council, chaired by Rabbi Porath and dated December 20, 1939, that stated that:

> The actual Kashruth situation remains the same as before, with no supervision of the retail meat markets leaving the way open to misrepresentation and fraud. . . . It is now clear that the Orthodox rabbis as a group are not seeking the assistance and cooperation of the Council and . . . some of them are in fact opposing it.[139]

However, the situation of kashrut in Cleveland was in the process of changing because in March 1940, Rabbi Porath reported to the annual meeting of the Jewish Community Council concerning a new rabbinic organization called the Orthodox Rabbinical Council (Merkaz ha-Rabbonim). This organization had somehow managed to achieve the unity that had eluded previous Orthodox rabbinical organizations in Cleveland. According to Rabbi Porath's report, the Merkaz now included all but one Cleveland Orthodox rabbi and that holdout

---

136 Clipping in KFA.

137 JW, November 4, 1934, 4. Cf. "Tsu di shuln, members, un president," JW, October 5, 1928.

138 "Vi azoi hot der merkaz ha-rabbonim bahandelt di kashrus frage letstn yor?" JW October 7, 1940.

139 Jewish Community Council, Report of the Committee on Kashruth, December 20, 1939, 2, KFA.

had also agreed to abide by its decisions. As a result, Rabbi Porath reported that rabbinical inspection of kosher establishments in the city had recommenced, and he advocated for the appointment of full-time mashgiḥim, the need for whom he felt was evident.[140]

Rabbi Porath, in an undated speech to the Union of Orthodox Jewish Congregations of America from a somewhat later date, describes the Merkaz ha-Rabbonim in this way:

> ... our locally organized Rabbinical Council [Merkaz ha-Rabbonim] ... consists of all Orth[odox] Rabbis in our community, elderly rabbis and younger ones. Some have come with a reputation from Europe, and others are American born. Some are members of Agudas ha-Rabbonim, others belong to the Histadrut [Rabbinical Council of America], and still others have their sympathies with the Hitaḥdut [Association of Rabbis of the United States and Canada]. Some belong to Agudat Israel, others to the Mizrahi, still others are independent. Though having different backgrounds, and philosophical outlooks, still with our differences of opinions and sympathies we are all working jointly as one united body, serving our community with one purpose in mind, namely the strengthening of Orthodox Judaism, and to enhance traditional observance. To my knowledge Cleveland is the only large city in the U.S. where such a united rabbinate has been conceived, and has been in existence for over two decades and functioning successfully.[141]

The successful functioning of this rabbinical body is evidenced by the fact that in 1941, the Merkaz ha-Rabbonim created a permanent rabbinical court (*bet din*) for the community, which was to have its sessions in both the Beth Midrash ha-Gadol synagogue on East 105th Street and the Educational Alliance on Kinsman Road, thus covering both major areas of Jewish population in the city.[142]

Developments in Cleveland Jewish Orthodoxy starting in 1941 will be discussed in the next chapter.

---

140 Copy of the report, dated March 18, 1941, KFA.
141 Undated, Rabbi Israel Porath Papers MSS 4753, WRHS, folder 8.
142 JW, December 29, 1941, KFA.

CHAPTER 2

The Evolution of the Orthodox Jewish Community in Cleveland, Ohio, 1941 to the Present

The establishment of the Orthodox Rabbinic Council (Merkaz ha-Rabbonim) in 1940, described in the previous chapter, enabled an historic partnership between that organization and the Cleveland Jewish Federation that created a basically stable and trustworthy foundation for kashrut in Cleveland lasting for several decades. In 1945, when Cleveland had sixty-seven kosher butchers,[1] the delicate and complex negotiations for this partnership began. As described by a Cleveland Jewish Federation official writing in 1975:

> Two years were spent in establishing the institution, convincing all sections of the community of its validity and the need for a communal underpinning, and convincing the butchers and the slaughterers and the shochtim that they could trust communal mashgichim under the joint supervision of the Orthodox Rabbinical Council and our Federation.[2]

The result in 1947 was a Kashruth Board, administered by the Jewish Community Council and the Orthodox Rabbinical Council.[3] The system basically worked, though it was certainly not foolproof. In 1963, Rabbi Shubert

---

1   Samuel G. Freedman, *Jew vs. Jew: the Struggle for the Soul of American Jewry* (New York: Simon and Schuster, 2000), 291.
2   Rabbi Shubert Spero Papers, WRHS MSS 3988 folder 8: October 20, 1975.
3   Vincent and Rubenstein, *Merging Traditions*, 57.

Spero (b. 1923) counted thirty-seven kosher butchers in Cleveland of whom ten, in his opinion, were personally Sabbath observant (*shomer Shabbat*) and thus absolutely reliable. He reported in a letter to a rabbi in Toronto that while

> the system [of kashrut] is effective . . . it is not foolproof. Should a butcher deliberately set out to sell traifa [non-kosher meat], I believe he could get away with it, for a time at least. To be on the safe side, all of "our" people and the public institutions (hospitals and the JCC) are instructed to buy from the Shomer Shabbos butchers.[4]

In 1986 the co-chairs of the Merkaz ha-Rabbonim, Rabbis Jacob Muskin (1920–1990)[5] and Isidore Pickholz (1918–2006)[6] could report that "Cleveland is one of few cities where all Orthodox rabbis have joined together in consensus," that the Merkaz was working together with Kashruth Board of the Jewish Community Federation, and that its Beth Din [religious court] was recognized by the Israel Chief Rabbinate.[7]

Postwar Orthodoxy in Cleveland

One of the first major issues facing Cleveland Jewry in the period after the end of World War II was the resettling of Jewish Holocaust survivors from Europe, many of whom came to Cleveland. Because the majority of the refugee survivors relocating in Cleveland were Orthodox (398 of 709 or 56.5%), in welcoming them to Cleveland, the Jewish community agencies involved in their reception had to take into consideration religious issues such as kashrut when attempting to provide housing, which was in short supply in postwar Cleveland.[8]

---

4   Rabbi Shubert Spero Papers, WRHS MSS 3988 folder 2: January 28, 1963.
5   On Rabbi Muskin, see "Finding Aid for the Jacob Muskin Papers," WRHS, accessed February 22, 2022, http://ead.ohiolink.edu/xtf-ead/view?docId=ead/OCLWHi0121.xml;query=;brand=default.
6   On Rabbi Pickholz, see Margi Herwald, "Beloved Orthodox Leader Rabbi Isidore Pickholtz dies at 88," CJN, September 29, 2006, accessed February 22, 2022, https://www.cleveland-jewishnews.com/archives/beloved-orthodox-leader-rabbi-isidore-pickholtz-dies-at-88/article_f7a383ff-1c61-5976-b7c3-be5a113cde34.html.
7   CJN, March 7, 1986, 9.
8   Helen L. Glassman, *Adjustment in Freedom: A Follow-Up Study of One Hundred Jewish Displaced Families* (Cleveland: United HIAS Service and Jewish Family Service Association, 1956), 33–34, 83.

Housing was far from the only problem the Orthodox newcomers posed. The Cleveland Jewish community also encountered problems of resettling a "large influx of religious functionaries whose affidavits and contracts had been supplied by religious schools and congregations in an effort to rescue these people from [Displaced Persons] camps,"[9] the leadership of the Jewish Family Service Association met with Cleveland's Orthodox lay leadership in order to have them share with the community the task of resolving these problems, and an Orthodox advisory committee was formed.[10]

Jewish Family Service's essential issue was that its primary goal was to make the newly arrived refugees self-supporting as soon as possible whereas the "religious functionaries" resisted accepting what to them was inappropriate employment. From the Jewish Family Service's perspective, Orthodox Jews in general, and Orthodox rabbis and rabbinical students in particular, seemed to constitute obstacles to the smooth operation of their programs to help the Jewish Displaced Persons arriving in Cleveland.[11] Alone, these newly arrived Orthodox survivors would likely not have been able to effectively resist Jewish Family Service pressure to accept the employment opportunities offered to them. However, in their struggle with the Jewish Family Service Association the newcomers had the important institutional backing of the Telshe Yeshiva.

The Telshe Yeshiva

In 1941, only three years after the New Haven Yeshiva of Cleveland ceased its struggles for existence, the Telshe Yeshiva was established in Cleveland on East 105th Street.[12] Its founders, Rabbis Elya Meir Bloch (1894–1955)[13] and Chaim

---

9   Sylvia Bernice Fleck Abrams, "Searching for a Policy: Attitudes and Policies of Non-Governmental Agencies Toward the Adjustment of Jewish Immigrants of the Holocaust Era, 1933–1953, as Reflected in Cleveland, Ohio" (PhD, Case Western Reserve University, Cleveland, 1988), 192.

10 Ibid., 229–230.

11 Ibid., 210.

12 Gartner, *History of the Jews of Cleveland*, 318; On the Telshe Yeshiva see Mordechai Gifter, "Yeshivat Telz," in *Mosdot ha-Torah be-Eiropah be-Vinyanam u-ve-Hurbanam*, ed. Samuel K. Mirsky (New York: Ha-Histadrut ha-Ivrit ba-America, 1956), 169–188. Cited in Adam S. Ferziger, *Centered on Study: Typologies of the American Community Kollel* (Ramat Gan: The Rappaport Center for Assimilation Research and Strengthening Jewish Vitality, the Faculty of Jewish Studies, Bar Ilan University, 2009), 22.

13 On Rabbi Bloch, see Chaim Dov Keller, "Reb Eliahu Meir Bloch," *Jewish Observer* 12, no. 7 (September 1977): 6–13.

Mordechai Katz (1894–1964),[14] chose Cleveland after having investigated conditions in the Jewish communities of Pittsburgh, Cincinnati and Detroit. The new Cleveland yeshiva began with ten students.[15]

Practically from the start the yeshiva and the newcomers to Cleveland it attracted seemed to be a thorn in the side of the Jewish Family Service Association. As Jewish Family Service director Rae C. Weil, stated in 1946:

> We already have a large number of extremely Orthodox people who have no opportunities in Cleveland and have not been able to make any kind of economic adjustment. . . . In most instances they have not fitted in well and have spent most of their time and energy trying to get to New York.[16]

The Cleveland agency's difficulties with the Telshe Yeshiva mirror the lack of understanding between the Americanized professionals and volunteers who controlled the community's resettlement apparatus and the yeshiva leaders.[17]

By 1947, the yeshiva had succeeded in attracting a student body of 150[18] while its leaders, Rabbis Bloch and Mordechai Gifter (1915–2001),[19] who had joined the staff in 1944, tried to obtain the funds their growing institution required. The yeshiva thus demanded maximum community support for as many students as it could for as long as possible. As Sylvia Abrams states, "the rabbis were not interested in understanding community process and the niceties of national-local agency relationships."[20] This brought them into sharp conflict with the Jewish Family Service Association, which was certainly "unused to refugees responding to policy in this manner."[21] In 1948, Jewish Family Service expressed its preference not to take "yeshiva" cases.[22]

While struggling for its existence and financial stability, the Telshe Yeshiva did two seemingly opposite things. At one and the same time it began a process of isolating itself from the general Cleveland Jewish community while

14 "Thousands Attend Rabbi Katz's Rites," *New York Times*, November 19, 1964, 39.
15 "A Different Kind of School," CJN, December 23, 1966, 19.
16 Abrams, "Searching for a Policy," 331.
17 Abrams, "Searching for a Policy," 213.
18 Vincent and Rubenstein, *Merging Traditions*, 224.
19 Binyamin Rose, "The Prince of America's Torah Renaissance: An Appreciation of Rav Mordechai Gifter, ztz"l, on his Tenth Yahrtzeit," *Mishpacha*, December 29, 2010, 33–34.
20 Abrams, "Searching for a Policy," 214–215.
21 Ibid., 216–218.
22 Ibid., 223.

also attempting, with some success, to exercise an influence on Cleveland Orthodoxy.

Separation from the community is symbolized by the yeshiva's choice of relocation from its original home in Cleveland's Glenville neighborhood. In the 1940s and 1950s, the Jews of Cleveland, who were then largely concentrated in the Glenwood and Kinsman areas, faced the prospect of relocating. For some Cleveland institutions and families, this was the second neighborhood relocation within a generation. In the words of Rabbi Porath in 1945, "We see once again how Jewish neighborhoods are abandoned and emptied."[23] While nearly all Cleveland Jews, individually and institutionally chose to relocate to the Heights area, the Telshe Yeshiva went literally in an entirely different direction. It purchased an estate in Wickliffe, Ohio, some ten miles to the Northeast of the Jewish community. The yeshiva broke ground for its new Wickliffe campus in August, 1955,[24] and formally opened the new campus, consisting of "21 ultramodern buildings on 57 acres of suburban Cleveland" in June, 1957.[25] Rabbi Porath stated at the dedication of the new campus: "And here they have achieved the unbelievable. From a humble and seemingly insignificant beginning over ten years ago, this yeshiva has recaptured its old glory. It ranks again as a first class and universally recognized Tora [sic] institution of very high caliber."[26]

While physically separating itself from the Cleveland Jewish community, the Telshe leadership nonetheless made a number of efforts to exercise its influence on the broader Orthodox community. These efforts yielded considerable success over a period of years. Dr. Julius Weinberg (1923–1984) of Cleveland State University, educated at the Telshe Yeshiva, observed in a 1965 interview that Cleveland Orthodoxy had become more literate and had a stronger voice in the community, a development which he attributed to the Telshe Yeshiva and its influence.[27]

---

23 Rabbi Israel Porath, "Der Tzveyter H̱urbn fun Klivlander Orthodoksishe Shuln," JW, March 28, 1945, 2. This article is translated in its entirety in chapter six of this volume.

24 "Gov. Lausche Dedicates New Campus of Telshe Yeshiva College," JTA, August 30, 1955, accessed January 26, 2015, http://www.jta.org/1955/08/30/archive/gov-lausche-dedicates-new-campus-of-telshe-yeshiva-college.

25 "Four-day Festival Marks Opening of New Campus of Telshe Yeshiva," JTA, June 20, 1957, accessed January 26, 2015, http://www.jta.org/1957/06/20/archive/four-day-festivalmarks-opening-of-new-campus-of-telshe-yeshiva.

26 Rabbi Israel Porath Papers WRHS MSS 4753, folder 8: undated.

27 Bernice Green, "A Historian's View of Cleveland Jewry Today," CJN, December 31, 1965. On Weinberg, see "Julius Weinberg Dead at 61," JTA, February 15, 1984, accessed February 22, 2022, https://www.jta.org/archive/julius-weinberg-dead-at-61.

What did the yeshiva's influence mean in practice? One initiative for the purpose of illustration was that of a Telshe faculty member, Rabbi Aizik Ausband (1915–2012), who arranged for the first regular supply of milk produced under Jewish supervision (*cholov yisroel*) in Cleveland, thus showing the way toward the trend to a stricter interpretation of kashrut in Cleveland, of which more will be said below.[28]

A Telshe organizational initiative within the Cleveland community was the "Orthodox Jewish Association" created in fall 1950. As a contemporary report states, this organization was founded:

> . . . for the purpose of strengthening Jewish religious activities in Cleveland. The Association expects to have among its members all Orthodox groups, synagogues and religious institutions. It will operate within the framework of the pattern set by the Jewish Community Council.[29]

A letter dated August 19, 1997 from Rabbi Shubert Spero to Rabbi Elazar Muskin fleshes out the context of the founding of this organization. Rabbi Spero stated:

> Shortly after my arrival in Cleveland I was called to a meeting with Rabbis E. M. Bloch and C. M. Katz . . . who told me that the Roshei Yeshiva did not wish to isolate themselves from the "city" but rather saw themselves as a part of the general community and, given the sad state of Orthodoxy, felt a religious obligation to work for the ideals of Torah. They added that with the arrival of us young "spirited" rabbis, there was an opportunity to work together . . . Towards that end it was agreed to set up a broader-based organization called "The Orthodox Jewish Association (OJA)" to which all sorts of organizations would be invited to join. This was to include educational organizations such as Telz, Hebrew Academy, Yeshivat Adath, service organizations such as the Mikveh Association, synagogues, and also

---

28 "Telshe Yeshiva Leader Rabbi Ausband Dead at 96," CJN, May 13, 2012, 50.

29 "Cleveland Orthodox Groups Form Association; to Operate Within Jewish Community Council," JTA, October 31, 1950, accessed January 26, 2015, http://www.jta.org/1950/10/31/archive/cleveland-orthodox-groups-form-association-to-operate-within-jewish-community-council.

Agudah and Mizrachi. This saved the Roshei Yeshiva (in their view) from having to "recognize" synagogues with dubious mechitzas or rabbis with dubious *smichas* (which they would have had to do had this been an organization of synagogues or of rabbis . . .). Telz had no problem "affiliating" with this OJA since all it implied was that the various collectives involved wished to further Orthodoxy.[30]

Orthodox Education

Perhaps the most important of all the Telshe initiatives was the October 1943 founding of the Hebrew Academy of Cleveland. Hebrew Academy became the first day school in the city, and was among the first to open outside the greater New York area. Cleveland Jewry, including its Orthodox community, had hitherto not embraced the day school concept as we have seen. Thus, the project of creating Hebrew Academy was by all accounts guided by the rabbis of the Telshe Yeshiva whose ideals, as an account of the Academy's twenty-fifth anniversary states "reflected only the earnest desires of a few leaders."[31] It is of some significance to note that Hebrew Academy opened on the initiative of the Telshe leadership and did not grow out of Yeshiva Adath Bnei Israel, which was a Cleveland Orthodox communal educational institution that remained resolutely Orthodox, but also no less resolutely committed to the previously regnant model of supplementary Jewish education. Hebrew Academy opened, somewhat ironically, in the basement of the Conservative Cleveland Jewish Center on East 105th Street with eleven students in kindergarten and grade one,[32] though in its later literature Hebrew Academy claimed twenty-four original students.[33] In its initial years, the leadership of the Hebrew Academy went door-to-door to recruit students.[34] The institution has grown in its seven

---

30 Elazar Muskin, "When Unity Reigned: Yom ha-Azma'ut 1954," *Hakira* 13 (2012): 51–52, accessed February 26, 2015, http://www.hakirah.org/Vol13Muskin.pdf.

31 "Hebrew Academy Marks 25 Years of Dynamic Community Service," CJN, February 7, 1969, 21.

32 "Hebrew Academy of Cleveland—'the Mayflower of the Torah World,'" CJN, March 8, 2013, 1.

33 Freedman, *Jew vs. Jew*, 305.

34 Sarah Reymond, "Hebrew Academy Head Dies at Age 89: Rabbi N.W. Dessler Was leader in Jewish Education" CJN October 4, 2011 https://www.clevelandjewishnews.com/archives/hebrew-academy-head-dies-at-age-89/article_95580de9-bbd2-5d57-b57f-44940dbef279.html [accessed February 23, 2022]

decades of development to over 900 students as of September 2014 with a staff of over 200.[35]

A most important step in the development of Hebrew Academy and, indeed, in the development of the relations between Orthodox and non-Orthodox Jews in Cleveland was the decision by the Cleveland Jewish Federation, starting in 1948, to support the school financially, long before such support among other American Jewish Federations became customary.[36] A 1948 Hebrew Academy report, perhaps created because of the demands of the Federation for information on the school as it considered its subsidy, shows that the Hebrew Academy then educated 155 children from kindergarten to grade seven, which had opened just that year, while it also housed an afternoon school teaching an additional 94 children on a budget of $70,000 for the Academy and $11,000 for the afternoon school.[37]

Since it was the only day school in Cleveland, Hebrew Academy initially served all segments of the traditional Jewish community. Thus, Rabbi Spero remarked in 1963: ". . . you have children of penniless refugees sitting next to children of truly affluent parents. You have a Chasidic child with earlocks next to the child of a Conservative rabbi."[38] Fairly soon, though, the Telshe Yeshiva founded its own high school that offered, in Rabbi Spero's words, "a bare minimum" with respect to secular studies,[39] and two teachers colleges—one for men and one for women—by 1961.[40]

The situation in which Hebrew Academy was the only elementary day school in Cleveland would not last beyond the 1970s. Pressure was brought to bear on the Academy from opposite sides of the Orthodox ideological spectrum. Many Hebrew Academy parents whose interpretation of Orthodoxy was more "Modern" than that of the Telshe Yeshiva or who were more pro-Israel than the Telshe Yeshiva leadership, had become restive as early as the 1960s. Thus, in a 1963 letter to Rabbi Shubert Spero, a Cleveland couple expressed their desire for a new day school in the following way: "Were the Hebrew

35   Ed Wittenberg, "Hebrew Academy to Buy Oakwood Country Club", CJN September 12, 2014, 1; Sue Hoffman, "Most Jewish Day Schools See Growth Pattern", CJN, February 14, 2014, 21.
36   Rabbi Shubert Spero Papers, WRHS MSS 3988 folder 8: October 20, 1975; Sidney Z. Vincent and Judah Rubenstein, *Merging Traditions—Jewish Life in Cleveland: a Contemporary Narrative, 1945-1975; a Pictorial Record, 1839-1975*, 54.
37   Rabbi Shubert Spero Papers, WRHS MSS 3988 folder 26: November 10, 1948.
38   Rabbi Shubert Spero Papers, WRHS MSS 3988 folder 2: January 16, 1963.
39   Rabbi Shubert Spero Papers, WRHS MSS 3988 folder 2: June 19, 1962.
40   Freedman, *Jew vs. Jew*, 305.

Academy not under the dominance of anti-Israel religious zealots of the Telshe yeshiva . . . many members of this community might not feel so pressing a need for an additional Hebrew day school."[41]

Indeed, one of the ways the Yeshiva's leadership exercised its influence on the Hebrew Academy was through the curricular de-emphasis of the importance of the State of Israel. Rabbi Elazar Muskin gives a cogent example:

> I vividly recall how in 1964, while I was in fourth grade [in HA], I was dismissed from my class by the teacher when I, asked to list Jewish holidays, included *Yom ha-Azma'ut* [Israel Independence Day] as one of them. My father . . . upset over this reaction, insisted that the teacher apologize to me and my father, which she was forced to do in front of the then principal of the school, Rabbi N.W. Dessler (1922–2011).[42]

In this connection, Muskin also states:

> It is interesting to note that a year later the Hebrew Academy of Cleveland ran a *Yom ha-Azma'ut* program in the school and featured it in a newsletter called "Inside the Hebrew Academy" vol. 1, no. 3, May, 1965 . . . The school never celebrated *Yom ha-Azma'ut* as a religious holiday; rather they recognized it as they did Thanksgiving, which also had its own assembly and performance.[43]

Muskin observes that within Cleveland's Orthodox community during this period there were "tremendous tensions" between the Telshe Yeshiva and the Hebrew Academy, which it practically controlled, and the religious Zionist community. Israel Independence Day was not celebrated at Telshe Yeshiva, and the Judaic Studies teachers at Hebrew Academy expressed negativity towards religious Zionism and its youth movement B'nai Akivah, echoing the yeshiva's attitude toward that co-ed religious Zionist group.[44]

---

41 Rabbi Shubert Spero Papers, WRHS MSS 3988 folder 3: November 15, 1963.

42 On Rabbi Dessler, see Sarah Reymond, "Hebrew Academy Head Dies at Age 89: Rabbi N.W. Dessler Was Leader in Jewish Education," CJN, October 4, 2011, accessed February 23, 2022, https://www.clevelandjewishnews.com/archives/hebrew-academy-head-dies-at-age-89/article_95580de9-bbd2-5d57-b57f-44940dbef279.html.

43 Muskin, "When Unity Reigned," 53.

44 Muskin, "When Unity Reigned," 52–53.

By 1975 dissatisfaction with the Hebrew Academy by parents who espoused Religious Zionism resulted in a petition to the school asking that:

> The religious validity of the State of Israel should be recognized by all members of the Jewish studies Department. Youngsters belonging to religious community youth groups under the supervision of Orthodox community rabbis should not be discriminated against or made to feel that they are less religiously committed than other students.[45]

The Hebrew Academy administration, despite numerous meetings, was unable to come up with a formula that would satisfy the pro-Zionist element in the school. Summing up the situation in 1987, Rabbi [Aharon Hersh] Fried, the principal of the school, admitted "that at the Hebrew Academy over the years the issue [of the meaning of the State of Israel and Zionism] has been skirted."[46]

But it was not only Zionism and Israel that upset the Hebrew Academy parent body in the 1970s. In that period the administration of the girls high school, Yavne, issued a notice in which it stated its strong opposition to its students wearing slacks not merely in school but also during afterschool hours and on weekends, as well as attending social events like birthday parties where boys would be present.[47]

Differing approaches to the issues of the relationship of Torah and science also provoked dissent in the 1970s. In those years The Hebrew Academy confronted widely differing reactions among its parent body to the school's curricula in the earth and life sciences in which the school policy was that "any unit whose theme was against Torah values is omitted." There were parents espousing right-wing Orthodox views who agreed with this policy and felt that "non-Torah" value systems "poison the child's mind," while other parents felt that "even to downplay (and certainly to ignore) such issues . . . is grossly irresponsible."[48] The parents of the "Yeshiva element" also opposed their children watching educational TV and a proposed compromise according to which

---

45 Rabbi Shubert Spero Papers, WRHS MSS 3988 folder 26: January 30, 1975.
46 "Orthodox Day Schools: Why Have Three?," CJN, May 29, 1987, 5.
47 Rabbi Shubert Spero Papers, WRHS MSS 3988 folder 8: October 28, 1975, December 6, 1978.
48 Rabbi Shubert Spero Papers, WRHS MSS 3988 folder 25: June 13, 1977, 2. For historical perspective on American Orthodox attitudes toward these issues, see Ira Robinson, "American Jewish Views of Evolution and Intelligent Design," *Modern Judaism* 27 (2007): 173–192; idem, "'Practically I Am a Fundamentalist': Twentieth-Century Orthodox Jews Contend

"yeshiva" children would be excused from watching educational TV programs in class stirred up other parents who were concerned that "an eventual two track system . . . based . . . solely upon religious sensitivity" would effectively destroy the "communal" character of the Hebrew Academy worse than if the yeshiva element were permitted to leave Hebrew Academy and create a school of their own.[49]

By the late 1970s and early 1980s, all of this dissatisfaction with Hebrew Academy culminated in the creation of two additional Orthodox day schools in Cleveland, one to the ideological "right" of the Academy and the other to its "left." The right-wing school, Mosdos Ohr ha-Torah, was founded in 1978 and perhaps reflected the concern of its parent body that the "modern Orthodox" children at the Hebrew Academy might negatively influence their children's beliefs. Beyond that, Mosdos parents desired an education for their children that more strongly emphasized the study of Judaic texts.[50] A few years later, in 1982, Beit Sefer Mizrachi, now known as Fuchs Mizrachi, was founded as "a Modern Orthodox, Zionist, college-preparatory day school."[51]

In the supplementary school sector, Yeshiva Adath Bnai Israel strongly held on to its Orthodox identity. In the 1950s, Yeshiva Adath was allowed to retain its independent status as an afternoon Hebrew school even though a 1954 study urged its merger with the Cleveland Hebrew Schools on the grounds of greater efficiency and economy, because of "intense opposition" by the Orthodox community.[52] In the early 1960s there was similar pressure on the part of the Cleveland Jewish Federation to merge the institution with a non-Orthodox supplementary Hebrew school.[53] The ultimate withdrawal of Federation support to Yeshiva Adath did not come until the 1990s and was, at that time, a sign that the school had almost completely lost its Orthodox student base in competition with the day schools.[54]

---

with Evolution and Its Implications," in *Jewish Tradition and the Challenge of Darwinism*, ed. Geoffrey Cantor and Marc Swetlitz (Chicago: University of Chicago Press, 2006), 71–88.

49 Rabbi Shubert Spero Papers, WRHS MSS 3988 folder 25: undated document.

50 "Orthodox Day Schools: Why Have Three?," CJN, May 29, 1987, 5.

51 Sue Hoffman, "Fuchs Mizrachi Celebrates Second Year in New Home," CJN, January 13, 2012.

52 Sidney Vincent, "Summary of Jewish Education Study in Cleveland, Ohio," AJYB 57 (1956): 228; Rabbi Shubert Spero Papers, WRHS MSS 3988 folder 8: October 20, 1975; Vincent and Rubenstein, *Merging Traditions*, 58.

53 Frank Rabinsky to Israel Porath, Rabbi Israel Porath papers, WRHS MSS 4526, folder 3; Rabbi Shubert Spero Papers, WRHS MSS 3988 folder 1: March 15, 1960.

54 Marcy Oster, "Federation Plans to Withdraw YABI Funding," CJN, June 11, 1993, 16.

Synagogues

In the 1940s the Jewish community that had been created around East 105th Street (Glenville) and in the Kinsman Road district found itself pressured to move once again. In the words of Rabbi Israel Porath in 1945, "We see once again how Jewish neighborhoods are abandoned and emptied." Rabbi Porath saw the situation both as a crisis and as an opportunity. He wrote that there was an urgent need for Cleveland Orthodox Jewry to take stock of itself in this transitional period. In particular, Rabbi Porath urged the synagogues not to repeat the previous mistake of rebuilding all existing synagogues separately in their new neighborhoods. Synagogues should try to combine their forces and establish an Orthodox bloc to influence the Jewish Community Council.[55] And indeed, in the spirit of Rabbi Porath's pleas, Cleveland's Jewish Community Council and Federation met with all the Orthodox synagogues to help them plan their eventual move to the Heights area.[56] Influence was exerted to effect synagogue mergers so as to establish large conglomerate congregations, like the Taylor Road Synagogue, which in that era was officially named "Temple Beth Sholom,"[57] the Heights Jewish Center, and the Warrensville Center Synagogue with a higher membership base. As a result of this planning, Taylor Road became in the 1950s a street central to the Orthodox community, which included the Hebrew Academy, several synagogues, kosher bakeries, and food stores.[58]

The example of the Warrensville Center Synagogue, dedicated in April 1959, will illustrate the process. It encompassed the Tetiever Ahavas Achim Anshe Sfard, Bnai Jacob Kol Israel (Kinsman Jewish Center) and N'vai Zedek with a combined membership of over 1,000 families.[59] As Rabbi Porath stated at the new synagogue's dedication, "The shifting of population from the city to the suburbs has changed the whole structure of our local Orthodox Jewry. Old and long-established congregations, which had existed for many scores of years in the old neighborhoods had to be reshaped through mergers."[60]

---

55 Rabbi Israel Porath, "Der tsveyter ḥurbn fun klivlander orthodoksishe shuln," JW, March 28, 1945, 2.
56 Sidney Z. Vincent, *Personal and Professional: Memoirs of a Life in Community Service* (Cleveland: Jewish Community Federation of Cleveland, 1982), 180.
57 Rabbi Shubert Spero Papers, WRHS MSS 3988 folder 2: July 25, 1962.
58 Vincent and Rubenstein, *Merging Traditions*, 20.
59 "Three Cleveland Orthodox Congregations Announce Merger," JTA, April 22, 1959, accessed January 26, 2015, http://www.jta.org/1959/04/22/archive/three-cleveland-orthodox-congregations-announce-merger.
60 Rabbi Israel Porath Papers, WRHS MSS 4753 folder 8.

More recent decades have seen the mid-century trend toward fewer and larger synagogues somewhat reversed due to a desire for smaller, more intimate prayer services. Cleveland Rabbi Lawrence Zierler observed this trend, known as "shtiebelization," as early as the 1990s, particularly along the Taylor Road corridor.[61]

Kashrut

As mentioned at the beginning of this chapter, the alliance between the Merkaz ha-Rabbonim and the Cleveland Jewish Federation, established in 1947, had stabilized the supervision of kashrut in the city for several decades, while the creation of the Kashruth Board alongside significant Federation support for the two Orthodox schools, the Hebrew Academy and Yeshivath Adath, also greatly helped to breach the walls of misunderstanding and mistrust that had historically separated Cleveland's Orthodox community from the Federation leadership.[62]

But stable kashrut supervision was not able to prevent basic changes in kashrut in Cleveland. There were new forces in consumer marketing that affected the consumption of kosher products. As well, there was an almost inevitable attrition among kosher butcher shops, that were often financially marginal, and that faced the choice of relocating in areas to which Jews in Cleveland were moving or closing. Moreover, the passing of an immigrant generation that tended to purchase kosher meat regardless of individuals' level of Judaic belief (or lack thereof) meant a gradual diminution of the number of kosher butchers in Cleveland. In 1947, at the formal inception of the Kashruth Board, there were sixty-three kosher butchers in Cleveland. This number declined to thirty-seven in 1963, to twelve in 1975, and to three by the first decade of the twenty-first century.[63]

More significantly, in the late 1970s the structure of Cleveland kashrut came under pressure from the more strictly observant part of the Orthodox

---

61 Rabbi Zierler's remarks were published in CJN, October 18, 1996, 20. On this trend in contemporary Orthodox Judaism, see Simcha Fishbane, *The Shtiebelization of Modern Jewry: Studies in Custom and Ritual in the Judaic Tradition: Social-Anthropological Perspectives* (Boston: Academic Studies Press, 2011).

62 Vincent, *Personal and Professional*, 109–110.

63 Vincent and Rubenstein, *Merging Traditions*, 8; Rabbi Shubert Spero Papers, WRHS MSS 3988 folder 2: letter of January 28, 1963; *The Cleveland Jewish Community's Personal and Business Directory* (Cleveland Heights: Heights Community Mikveh, 2004), 106.

community that looked to institutions like the Telshe Yeshiva for guidance and that desired the new "gold standard" of kashrut supervision—constant onsite supervision—in contrast with the in-and-out inspection of two itinerant *mashgihim* that was the Kashruth Board's norm.[64] As Rabbi Abraham Berger stated in a 1978 letter to the *Cleveland Jewish News*: "To put it bluntly, the Orthodox community does not have confidence in the present mode of supervision."[65] Thus, forces within the Orthodox community, which by the 1970s constituted the core consumer group for kosher meat, had eroded confidence in the kosher butcher shops that continued to adhere to kashrut standards that had hitherto been considered adequate. This process culminated in 1990 when Irving's Meat Market closed. Irving's had been one of the last of the old-style kosher meat markets that had non-*shomer Shabbat* (Sabbath-observant) ownership and that had resisted the more stringent kashrut regulations including *glatt kosher*, the soaking and salting of all meat, and the installation of a permanent *mashgiah* on site.[66]

In 1993 Cleveland Jews witnessed the founding of the Va'ad ha-Kashrut of Cleveland. The Va'ad ha-Kashrut constituted a joint venture of the Merkaz ha-Rabbonim and the Jewish Community Federation. But, unlike the previous rabbinical-Federation partnership that had underpinned the Kashruth Board, the Va'ad ha-Kashrut was the result of the Cleveland Federation's desire to phase out its nearly half a century of support for the structure of kashrut in Cleveland. The Va'ad's end came in 1998, almost simultaneously with the end of Federation funding, and its demise was accompanied by the effective end of the Merkaz ha-Rabbonim as well.[67] Replacing the Va'ad ha-Kasshrut were no less than three kashrut organizations: Cleveland Kosher led by Rabbi Naftali Burnstein of the Young Israel Synagogue, Reliable Kashrut led by the last head of the Merkaz ha-Rabbonim, Rabbi Doniel Schur (1925–2006),[68] and the Vaad ha-Rabbonim ha-Chareidim led by Rabbi Yehuda Blum.[69]

---

64 "Report Says Consumers Get Fair Value in Kosher Meat," CJN, October 8, 1976, 10.

65 Abraham Berger, "Time to Improve Kashrut Picture," CJN, September 15, 1978, 55.

66 Bernice Green, "Irving's Meat Market Inc. Yields Kashrut Certification under Rabbinical Pressure," CJN, April 13, 1990, 3.

67 Marcy Oster, "Single Kashrut Standard is Not Attainable Here, VKC Steps Aside as Sole Kashrut Supervisory Authority," CJN, July 3, 1998, 3. Cf. "New Kashrut Board for New Era in Kashrut," CJN, December 31, 1993, 13; Marcy Oster, "Some Merchants Reluctant to Join Local Kashrut Group," CJN, December 2, 1994, 3.

68 On Rabbi Schur, see Margi Herwald, "Rabbi Schur, Advocate for Orthodoxy, Dies at 81," CJN, March 23, 2006, accessed February 23, 2022, https://www.clevelandjewishnews.com/archives/rabbi-schur-advocate-for-orthodoxy-dies-at-81/article_0c9cbe33-f31f-5cfe-afad-aaa268d85fa3.html.

69 Marcy Oster, "Kashrut Organizations Spring Up in Cleveland," CJN, June 25, 1999, 22.

Relations with Non-Orthodox Jews

In the early postwar period, the involvement of the Cleveland Jewish Federation in the organization of kashrut and in the financing of the Hebrew Academy was designed to facilitate a rapprochement between the Orthodox community in Cleveland and those non-Orthodox elements that supported Federation. However, some negative attitudes on the part of Cleveland's non-Orthodox Jews toward Orthodoxy did not change. The Jewish Family Service in the 1950s, for instance, tended to view the cohort of largely Orthodox Holocaust survivors in Cleveland with some patronization, and an opinion was expressed that for a number of the survivors, sending their children to the Orthodox day school was likely to change "as soon as they have moved into better neighborhoods."[70] Moreover, by the 1950s the growing political and societal power of the ultra-Orthodox, not merely in Israel but also in the United States, was apparent to prominent Cleveland Reform Rabbi Abba Hillel Silver. When, in a 1958 sermon, Silver criticized an American ultra-Orthodox leadership that avoided cooperation with other streams of Judaism, he was likely thinking of the local Orthodox leadership as well.[71]

Orthodox leaders at times publicly advocated political positions that were the opposite of those taken by the Federation leadership. Thus, in 1961 Cleveland Orthodox rabbis spoke out in favor of federal aid to parochial schools, despite the fact that, as Federation executive Sidney Vincent (1912–1982) stated, "The Federation overwhelmingly repeated its traditional support of the separation principle [between church and state]."[72] In the same year, the Orthodox rabbinate also expressed its dissatisfaction at the proposal that the newly built Jewish Community Center in Cleveland Heights would be open on Saturdays.[73]

As well, there was a persistent discomfort on the part of some Jews who identified with Federation with Orthodoxy's perceived negative views toward

---

70 Glassman, *Adjustment in Freedom*, 57–58.
71 Ofer Shiff, *The Downfall of Abba Hillel Silver and the Foundation of* Israel (Syracuse: Syracuse University Press, 2014), 46–47. It is noteworthy in this connection that Rabbi Silver donated $500.00 toward the publication of Rabbi Porath's book. Abba Hillel Silver to Israel Porath, November 17, 1954, Israel Porath Papers, WRHS 1, folder 2.
72 Sidney Vincent, "Cleveland: City without Jews," in *Remembering: Cleveland's Jewish Voices*, ed. Sally H. Wertheim and Alan D. Bennett (Kent: Kent State University Press, 2011), 74. On Vincent, see "Sidney Z. Vincent," *New York Times*, October 8, 1982, section A, 28.
73 Rabbi Shubert Spero Papers MSS 3988 WRHS, folder 32: August 9 and August 29, 1961.

non-Orthodox Judaism. In this vein, a Federation executive wrote Rabbi Shubert Spero on January 17, 1963:

> I consider Orthodoxy a valuable and noble expression of Jewish life . . . Does Orthodoxy reciprocate the respect? Can it, when it has such profound reservations about Reform and Conservatism as to create problems every time we plan so simple an event as an annual meeting at a Conservative synagogue?[74]

Federation executive Sidney Vincent, trying to be somewhat even handed, stated that:

> Federations often feel that the Orthodox community is needlessly difficult and has not yet pulled its weight in attaining crucial communal goals. The Orthodox community often thinks it is treated as a kind of communal stepchild, whose needs are viewed as nuisances to be accommodated as cheaply as possible.[75]

It remains a fact that through the 1970s only two Cleveland Federation Agencies: The Bureau of Jewish Education and the Jewish Family Service had an Orthodox president.[76]

In the 1980s, the Orthodox community had a considerable public relations problem on its hands concerning its initiative to create a community *eruv*.[77] This initiative drew opposition from the rest of the community as evidenced when a correspondent, who identified himself as a Conservative Jew, wrote to Rabbi Spero in 1982, combining the *eruv* issue with other perceived Orthodox irritants: "I differ with you and object strongly to your proposal to create an Eruv in my community. I disapprove of mezuzah inspections, mitzvoth vans, and proselization [sic] in attempts to get me to follow your standards of observance."[78]

---

74 Rabbi Shubert Spero Papers, WRHS MSS 3988 folder 2: January 17, 1963.
75 Vincent, *Personal and Professional*, 274; Vincent and Rubenstein, *Merging Traditions*, 58.
76 Vincent and Rubenstein, *Merging Traditions*, 58.
77 An *eruv* is a symbolic demarcation of a boundary that allows Orthodox Jews to carry objects on the Sabbath. On the often contentious history of the *eruv* in North America, see Adam Mintz, *Building Communities: The History of the Eruv in America* (Boston: Academic Studies Press, 2023).
78 Rabbi Shubert Spero Papers, WRHS MSS 3988 folder 9: October 21, 1982. For an example of the opposition raised by an *eruv* in the Montreal suburb of Outremont, Québec, see Valerie Stoker, "Drawing the Line: Hasidic Jews, Eruvim, and the Public Space of Outremont, Quebec," *History of Religions* 43, no. 1 (2003): 18–49.

The feeling of alienation from Orthodoxy on the part of Cleveland's non-Orthodox Jews in the 1990s was hardly assuaged when the *mikveh* (ritual pool) located on Lee Road in Cleveland Heights, which had been available for non-Orthodox conversions to Judaism, was closed and those in charge of its replacement were not receptive to such conversions. This meant that non-Orthodox conversions were forced, at least temporarily, to utilize a *mikveh* in Youngstown, Ohio, approximately seventy-five miles away.[79]

Tensions really came to a head in the late 1990s when several Orthodox institutions, including the Young Israel Synagogue, the Yavne High School of the Hebrew Academy, and Chabad, wanted to relocate on a stretch of South Green Road in Beachwood where the Green Road Synagogue was already located. The bitterly contested fight over the municipal zoning variation needed to make this project a reality, which pitted the non-Orthodox and the Orthodox Jews against each other, has been described in detail by Samuel G. Freedman.[80] In this connection I will note only that even Reform Rabbi Joshua Aaronson, who ultimately supported the zoning variance that would make it possible for the Orthodox institutions to locate on Green Road, prefaced his support of this plan in a key High Holidays sermon with the words: "In truth the behavior of the Orthodox has been unseemly at best. The Orthodox supporters of the Green Road campus have been unwilling to compromise and have engaged in scare tactics."[81]

The Orthodox Community in Cleveland Today

The Orthodox Jewish community in Cleveland at the beginning of the twenty-first century is an increasingly important part of the Jewish community as a whole. The Cleveland Jewish population has remained relatively stable over the last few years, according to the 2011 Greater Cleveland Jewish Population Study. The study found some 80,800 Jews living in the greater Cleveland area, down slightly from 81,500 in 1996. This means that in the past twenty years the Jewish population of Cleveland has remained relatively stagnant. In contrast, the study found that the Orthodox community grew during that period

79 Freedman, *Jew vs. Jew*, 317. Cf. Marcy Oster, "Last Towel in Place for New Community Mikveh," CJN, May 27, 1994, 27; idem, "Lee Road Mikveh to Remain Closed—Roof Collapsed," CJN, January 17, 1997, 4.

80 Freedman, *Jew vs. Jew*, 284–337.

81 Ibid., 324.

by 2,200.[82] This means that Orthodox Jews now constitute 18% of Cleveland Jewry, as opposed to 14% in 1996 and 8.9% in 1980, and, significantly, they constitute fully 33% of young adults (18–34), though only 10% of the sample of those of all ages who self-identified with a religious denomination.[83] The increasing demographic importance of the Orthodox community within Cleveland Jewry means that anyone at all interested in the present and future of the Cleveland Jewish community must get to know these people.

We have an important tool with which to begin our thinking about Cleveland Orthodoxy at the beginning of the twenty-first century. The Cleveland Mikveh Association has been issuing an annual directory for approximately the past two decades. In 1994, this Mikveh Association publication listed 1174 Orthodox households in Cleveland.[84] A decade later, in 2004, the directory listed 1445 families, as well as 177 businesses of various sorts,[85] fully substantiating the Cleveland Jewish population survey's findings of an increase in the Orthodox community.

The following observations are based on an examination of the 2004 directory, which is concerned with more than rabbis[86] and synagogues.[87] The first thing that seems particularly noteworthy is the emphasis placed in the directory on Torah study. Thus, the directory lists not merely "schools"[88] but also Torah "Learning Opportunities,"[89] and fully four pages of "Shiurim/ Classes," ranged by time from 6:00 a.m. on Sunday to 9:00 p.m. on Saturday night, including as well a small number (fifteen) of designated "Women's Classes."[90] Insofar as the Orthodox community's reality approaches the image portrayed in the directory, it is a community that thrives on schools and other educational opportunities for Jews of all ages.

---

82 Marcy Oster, "Survey of Cleveland Jewry Finds Stable Population," January 25, 2012, accessed January 26, 2015, http://www.jta.org/2012/01/25/news-opinion/united-states/survey-of-cleveland-jewry-finds-stable-population.

83 "2011 Greater Cleveland Jewish Population Study," Jewish Federation of Cleveland, January 24, 2012, accessed February 23, 2015, http://issuu.com/jcfcleve/docs/5818_population_study_feb7/1. Cf. "Distribution of Jewish Population—1970 and 1980," Rabbi Shubert Spero Papers WRHS MSS 3988 folder 23.

84 Marcy Oster, "Last Towel in Place for New Community Mikveh," CJN, May 27, 1994, 21.

85 The Cleveland Jewish Community's Personal and Business Directory.

86 Fifteen rabbis are listed. Ibid., 3.

87 Twenty-one synagogues are listed. Ibid., 4.

88 The only non-Orthodox institution listed is the former Siegal College of Judaic Studies. Ibid., 13.

89 Ten institutions are listed. Ibid., 13.

90 Ibid., 16–19.

The contemporary Cleveland orthodox community has embraced the idea that a day school education is a "must" for living a fully Orthodox life. Supplementary Jewish education backgrounds as well as the presence of not fully observant Jews in Orthodox life seems to be a waning phenomenon in Cleveland as in most North American Orthodox communities.[91] This Orthodox reliance on day school education has been partially supported and enabled by the Cleveland Jewish Federation, which, in its 2014 allocation, gave $474,791 to the Fuchs-Mizrachi School and $1,216,269 to the Hebrew Academy.[92]

It is noteworthy that a significant portion of the Cleveland Orthodox community derives its employment from Jewish education. In 2014, Hebrew Academy had a staff of 212 for some 900 students, Mosdos Ohr Hatorah had 98 on staff to serve 487 students and Fuchs Mizrachi listed 93 staff people for 461 students.[93] This works out to over 400 staff people among the three Orthodox day schools combined, a fairly consistent ratio of students to staff of less than five to one. To the number of Cleveland Orthodox Jews engaged in Jewish education must be added the staff at the Telshe Yeshiva, which has experienced a declining enrollment, claiming about 130 students (including approximately 80 in the high school) in 2013, down from approximately 400 in 1967.[94] The number also does not count Orthodox community educational outreach institutions like the *kollelim*.

Adam Ferziger has examined two of the most important educational outreach *kollelim* in the Cleveland Orthodox community. One of them, headed by Rabbi Yankel Zev Katz, began in the 1980s as a *kollel meḥankhim* (a *kollel* for teachers) in Cleveland Heights. Male Orthodox day school teachers were invited to study Torah for two hours daily, and received a small stipend to supplement their often inadequate salaries. In the 1990s, Rabbi Katz transformed his institution into a full-time community *kollel*, moving it to Beachwood and University Heights so as not to compete with an existing Haredi community *kollel* in Cleveland Heights. Katz Kollel members received a fellowship of $22,000 a year for studying Talmudic texts during the day and sharing their learning with community members in the evening. These activities, as well

91 Jeffrey Gurock addresses this phenomenon in his article "The Winnowing of American Orthodoxy," in his *American Jewish Orthodoxy in Historical Perspective* (Hoboken, NJ: KTAV, 1996), 299–312.

92 "Dollars at Work," Cleveland Jewish Federation, October 23, 2014, accessed February 23, 2015, http://issuu.com/jcfcleve/docs/1312_web_version_alloc-story/0.

93 Sue Hoffman, "Most Day Schools See Growth Patterns," CJN, February 14, 2014, 21; Ed Wittenberg, "HA to Buy Oakwood Country Club," CJN, September 12, 2014, 1.

94 Ed Wittenberg, "Telshe Yeshiva Hidden Gem in Lake County," CJN, August 23, 2013.

as the *kollel's* more popular lectures, have as their ultimate goal to strengthen the "yeshivish" element in the University Heights/Beachwood Orthodox community.[95]

Cleveland's Torat Tzion Kollel presented an alternate, more Israel-centered vision of Orthodoxy, aiming at the local modern Orthodox community. It began in 1994 through the efforts of Bob Stark, who provided some $250,000 annually to bring rabbis as well as students from a prominent Israeli yeshiva, Har Etzion, to establish a study hall in the Fuchs Mizrachi School as a base for advancing their own Talmudic erudition and for a wide variety of formal and informal educational activities with the student body. In addition, this *kollel* created another study hall in Beachwood's Young Israel Synagogue to offer opportunities for Torah learning to the larger Orthodox community in the evenings and on weekends. This *kollel* seems to have filled a need in Cleveland's modern Orthodox community.[96]

Ferziger notes that:

> While the Haredi world's activities emanate from increased strength and self-confidence, the development of the Israeli kollels is part of Modern Orthodoxy's response to a "crisis" that it has experienced since the 1980s. Many products of Modern Orthodox homes and schools have found the Haredi approach far more attractive and fulfilling than their parent's version. Conversely, others have responded to their uninspiring upbringings by abandoning religious observance altogether. The Israeli Religious-Zionist community as such—with its "battle-hardened" Sabra Torah students—has been drafted as one possible cure to the ideological malaise and lack of passionate role models that has become endemic to this sector of American Orthodoxy.[97]

While the Torat Tzion Kollel marked an attempt to counter the "yeshivish" tone of Cleveland orthodox life, the public face of the community, as portrayed in its publications like the Mikveh Directory and by a website entitled "Local Jewish News: News for the Cleveland Orthodox Jewish Community,"[98]

---

95 Ferziger, "Centered on Study," 22–24.
96 Ibid., 51–52. Cf. Freedman, *Jew vs. Jew*, 324.
97 Ferziger, "Centered on Study," 53.
98 "Local Jewish News," accessed February 25, 2015, http://www.localjewishnews.com.

maintains a quite distinct "yeshivish" atmosphere. Characteristic of this is the network of communal self-help organizations known collectively as *gemach*.[99] The current Cleveland *gemach* list is a nine-page document that describes dozens of different types of goods and services available to the community at little or no cost. These *gemachs* range from food to clothing to medical equipment and much more.[100]

At the beginning of the twenty-first century, the Orthodox Jewish community in Cleveland seems to be thriving. Its main current challenge, however, must be considered with great seriousness. It is a growing community in the midst of a larger Jewish community that is demographically stagnant. Historically, the institutions of the Cleveland Orthodox community have existed and thrived because they were supported not merely by the committed Orthodox but by the larger community. Synagogues, kosher stores, and Hebrew book shops alike often depend at least partially on general community patronage. The large number and variety of institutions that support Orthodox Jewish life in Cleveland would not be there in the same way without this wider patronage. What will become of that wider patronage in a community where the non-Orthodox sector is shrinking?

Because Cleveland Orthodoxy is a community in which the ideal of Torah study means that a significant portion of the community is either not gainfully employed or underemployed, its institutions even now find it hard to make ends meet. Thus, for example, Hebrew Academy had in the 2014/5 fiscal year a budget of over $8 million, with over seventy percent of the student body on full or partial scholarships. Even factoring in a $1.2 million Federation subsidy, Hebrew Academy finds itself needing to raise over $2 million to close its budgetary gap.[101] Will Hebrew Academy and its sister institutions in the Cleveland Orthodox community find the economic resources they require to survive and thrive in the twenty-first century? Will the larger Jewish community of Cleveland continue to support its institutions to the same degree? Like all good questions pertaining to the future, this one yields no clear and unambiguous answer.

---

99   This is a Hebrew acronym for *gemilut ḥasadim*—"works of kindness."

100 "Local Jewish News," accessed February 25, 2015, http://www.localjewishnews.com/wp-content/uploads/2014/10/Cleveland-Gemach-List-v-2.0.pdf.

101 Hebrew Academy fundraising letter, January 18, 2015. Copy in the possession of the author.

CHAPTER 3

Hasid and Maskil: The Hasidic Tales of a Cleveland Yiddish Journalist[1]

> If a Hasid says, "I have seen [it] with my eyes,"
> maybe he has heard [the story].
> And when he says he heard [it],
> it certainly never happened.
> —Rabbi Hayyim Halberstam of Sanz[2]

When Samuel Rocker died in 1936 at the age of seventy-one,[3] he was the publisher of a Yiddish-language daily newspaper in Cleveland, Ohio, entitled the *Yiddishe Velt* (*Jewish World*). As such, he was a person who possessed significant power and influence with the members of the Eastern European immigrant Jewish community of Cleveland who were his readers. For those interested in gaining influence within that community, including the leaders of the establishment of the Cleveland Jewish community, as well as for Ohio politicians who sought the *Yiddishe Velt*'s electoral support, Rocker was a man to be reckoned with.[4]

---

1   I would like to thank Professors Justin Jaron Lewis and Steven Engler, from whose comments on an earlier draft of this article I learned much.

2   Zvi Moshkovits, *Kol ha-Katuv le-Ḥayyim* (Jerusalem, 1962), 6.

3   On Rocker, see *Encyclopedia Judaica* (Ramat Gan: Keter, 1970), vol. 14, col. 213, and an obituary in the *New York Times*, March 19, 1936, 25. Cf. Joseph Shapiro, *Morai u-Meḥankhai: Zikhronot, Reshamim, Ḥavayot* (Tel-Aviv: Netiv, 1972), 123–133.

4   Lloyd Gartner, *History of the Jews of Cleveland* (Cleveland: Western Reserve Historical Society, 1978), 214–215, 225–226; Baruch Zuckerman, *Zikhronos* (New York: Farlag Yiddisher Kempfer, 1962), vol. 1, 155.

If that were all we knew about Rocker, we would most probably characterize him simply as a modernizing force within the Jewish community. For it is commonplace for observers of the North American Yiddish press of the early twentieth century to view it as an "Americanizing agency." It was thus an important link in a process of acculturation whereby Eastern European Jews acclimatized themselves to America and its way of life while retaining important linguistic and cultural ties to their past.[5] Rocker, as publisher of *Yiddishe Velt*, certainly fulfilled this expectation. However the writing of newspaper editorials and essays, which caused him to be remembered as a "Yiddish Walter Lipmann,"[6] was only part of his contribution to the acculturation process of Eastern European Jewish immigrants. For beyond his persona of "Samuel Rocker," American Yiddish journalist, he was also "Reb Yehoshua [Joshua] Rocker,"[7] author of a book on the Talmudic interpretation of the Bible[8] as well as two books of Hasidic tales.[9] This means that Rocker served as a cultural

---

5   Mordecai Soltes, "Yiddish Press: an Americanizing Agency," AJYB (1924–1925): 165–372; Moses Rischin, *The Promised City: New York Jews, 1870–1914* (Cambridge, MA: Harvard University Press, 1972), chapter 7; Leon Stein, Abraham Conan, and Lynn Davison, trans., *The Education of Abraham Cahan* (Philadelphia: Jewish Publication Society of America, 1969); Ronald Sanders, *The Downtown Jews: Portrait of an Immigrant Generation* (New York: Harper and Row, 1969); Isaac Metzker, ed., *A Bintel Brief: Sixty Years of Letters from the Lower East Side to the Jewish Daily Forward* (Garden City: Doubleday, 1971). There is relatively little on the "provincial" North American Yiddish press of that era. Cf. David Rome and Pierre Anctil, *Through the Eyes of the Eagle: the Early Montreal Yiddish Press (1907–1916)* (Montréal: Véhicule Press, 2001); and David Rome, "Men of the Yiddish Press," *Canadian Jewish Archives* n.s. 42 (1989). On *Yiddish Velt* itself, see Shapiro, *Morai*, 123–128.

6   Gartner, *History of the Jews of Cleveland*, 214.

7   Yehoshua (Joshua) was apparently Rocker's original name. Samuel/Joshua Rocker was far from the only Jew in North America to adopt a personal name different from his name of origin. For example, Shneur Zalman Schechter, president of the Jewish Theological Seminary of America, changed his given name to Solomon when he arrived in the Western world. Cf. Norman Bentwich, *Solomon Schechter: A Biography* (Philadelphia: Jewish Publication Society of America, 1948). A North American immigrant rabbi of the same era, Rabbi Yeshaiah (Isaiah) Glazer, used Simon as his given name. On Glazer, see Robinson, *Rabbis and Their Community*, chapter 3. Possibly, Samuel was chosen because it somewhat corresponded to the Galician/Ukrainian/Hungarian pronunciation of Yehoshua, "Shia."

8   Joshua Rocker, *Sefer Divrei Ḥakhamim: Derashot Ḥazal mi-Talmud Bavli, milukatim mi-kol ha-mekomot asher hema mifuzarim, u-mesudarin be-seder nakhon 'al mikraot ha-Tora. Mizuraf le-zeh sefer avnei ḥefets: devarim yekarim ve-neḥmadim, mi-sefarim rishonim ve-aḥaronim le-varer ule-laben maamarim temoḥim ve-amukim* (Cleveland: Rocker Printing Company, 1919). The book was first printed in 1903, according to the title page. The 1919 edition is available at the website www.hebrewbooks.org.

9   The first of these books is Rocker's *Der Sanzer Tsaddik: R. Hayyim Halberstam, zts"l di vunderbare lebens-geshikhte fun dem Sanzer tsaddik, velkher iz aroys fun a mitnagdishe svive, zu veren eyner fun di greste gute yidden in zayn dor: zayn leben. zayn virken. zayne taten, zayn tetigkeit in ḥasidus, zayn geonus in nigleh un nistar biz di moradige maḥlokes Sanz un Sadagure,*

mediator not simply between the Eastern European Jewish immigrants and their new country, but also between these immigrant Jews and their religious past. This past included the study of the Talmud as a highly valued religious and cultural activity,[10] as well as the religious traditions embodied in the stories that he told about the great masters of the Hasidic movement. It is his construction of the Hasidic tradition in his books that will mostly concern us in this chapter.

It is important for us, at the outset, to clearly understand that the Hasidic tradition evoked in Rocker's books, concerns a movement in Judaism, which emerged in the eighteenth century in Eastern Europe and played an important, if sometimes paradoxical, role in the process of the modernization of Eastern European Jews.[11] It is equally important for us to understand that the presentation of the Hasidic tradition in the form of collections of Hasidic stories concerning the movement's great spiritual leaders was largely a function of the late nineteenth and early twentieth centuries, a product of the clash between Hasidic Judaism and several competitive ideologies of that period, which included Europeanization (*haskala*), socialism, and Zionism.[12] It thus constitutes an example of Eric Hobsbawm's thesis that the period 1870–1914 witnessed not merely the overthrow of many premodern lifestyles, but also the "invention" of a number of national and ethnic "traditions."[13] Finally, it is worth noting that, in a number of cases, collections of Hasidic stories were edited and published

---

dertseylt zum ersten mol in a reyn yiddishe shprakh (Vienna: Union Buchdruckerei for Hayyim Zvi Heshe Kauftel [New York], 5687 [1926/7], repr. Bnei Brak, 5730 [1969/70]). This book is also available at www.hebrewbooks.org. The second book is Rocker's *Toldos Anshei Shem: Di lebens-geshikhte fun dem gaon u-mekubal R. Shneur Zalman Ladier, di ungarishe geonim R. Moshe Teitlboym, R. Yekutiel Yehuda Teitlboym, un andere tsaddikim; zeyr leben, zeyr virken, zayere taten, zayr tetigkeit in ḥasidus, zayr geonus in nigle un nistar, dertseylt zum ershten mol in a reyn yiddisher shprakh* (Cleveland: Progressive Printing Company, 5699 [1939]). Kauftel was Rocker's brother-in-law. Cf. Rocker, *Toldos Anshei Shem*, 5.

10 Jacob Katz, *Tradition and Crisis: Jewish Society at the End of the Middle Ages* (New York: Schocken, 1971), chapter 18; Mark Zborowski, and Elizabeth Herzog, *Life Is With People: The Culture of the Shtetl* (New York: Schocken, 1962).

11 Gershon David Hundert, *Jews in Poland-Lithuania in the Eighteenth Century: A Genealogy of Modernity* (Berkeley: University of California Press, 2004), chapter 9; Shaul Magid, *Hasidism on the Margin: Reconciliation, Antinomianism, and Messianism in Izbica/Radzin Hasidism* (Madison: University of Wisconsin Press, 2004).

12 Ira Robinson, "Hasidic Hagiography and Jewish Modernity," in *Jewish History and Jewish Memory: Essays in Honor of Yosef Haim Yerushalmi*, ed. Elisheva Carlebach, John M. Efron, and David N. Myers (Hanover: University Press of New England, 1998), 405–412; Justin Jaron Lewis, *Imagining Holiness: Classic Hasidic Tales in Modern Times* (Montreal: McGill-Queen's University Press, 2009).

13 Eric Hobsbawm, "Mass-Producing Traditions: Europe, 1870–1914," in *The Invention of Tradition*, ed. E. Hobsbawm and T. Ranger (Cambridge: Cambridge University Press, 1983), 263–307.

by people who were not themselves committed Hasidic Jews in the full sense and whose relationship to Hasidic Judaism could sometimes be described as ambivalent.[14] Rocker himself was such an ambivalent presenter of Hasidic tales, as we shall soon see.

He was born in 1864 or 1865 in Gorlice, southern Poland, then part of the Austro-Hungarian Empire. His father, usually referred to as Reb Ephraim Fishel Gorlitser, was a fervent Hasid and Talmudic scholar, who held the position of *dayyan* (judge of the rabbinical court) attached to the retinue of Rabbi Hayyim Halberstam (1793–1876), the Hasidic leader of Sanz (now Nowy Sącz).[15] Growing up in a strongly Hasidic environment, Joshua Rocker was able to personally visit several Hasidic courts in Galicia and Hungary,[16] and was educated in the Hasidic tradition both formally and informally. As he matured, however, while he remained an observant Orthodox Jew,[17] he drew away somewhat from his initial strong attachment to Hasidism, as did many of his contemporaries, through his exposure to the writings of the nineteenth-century Jewish movement for Europeanization, the *haskala*.[18] Thus he recounted how, even as a young man in Europe, when he celebrated the Sabbath in the same town as the son and successor of Rabbi Hayyim Halberstam, Rabbi Yechezkele of Siniewa, he did not go to visit him, as a normal Hasid would have done, "because," he related, "my Hasidism had even then evaporated [*oysgevefte*]."[19]

Rocker emigrated to the United States in 1891, and established the first Jewish print shop in Cleveland in 1898. He simultaneously began a career in Yiddish journalism in Cleveland, which culminated in his becoming editor, and,

---

14 Joseph Dan, "A Bow to Frumkinian Hasidism," *Modern Judaism* 11 (1991): 175–193. Lewis, in his "Imagining Holiness," expresses doubt concerning Dan's thesis.

15 He is described in a Sanzer source as "a great sage [*talmid ḥakham*]." Moshkovits, *Kol ha-Katuv le-Ḥayyim*, 57. Cf. Rocker, *Der Sanzer Tsaddik*, 15, 52, 101.

16 Rocker, *Der Sanzer Tsaddik*, 51, 149, 159; idem, *Toldos Anshei Shem*, 147, 161, 209.

17 Thus, Rabbi Max Wohlgelernter in a letter dated March 24, 1936 described Rocker at the time of his death as a person "who both in his personal life as well as in his communal and journalistic activities was a true exponent and staunch defender of Orthodoxy." Rocker Papers, Western Reserve Historical Society, Cleveland, Ohio.

18 Shapiro, *Morai*, 124. On the *haskala* movement, see Michael Stanislawski, *For whom do I toil?: Judah Leib Gordon and the Crisis of Russian Jewry* (New York: Oxford University Press, 1988); Raphael Mahler, *Hasidism and Haskalah in Galicia and the Congress Kingdom of Poland in the First Half of the Nineteenth Century* [Hebrew] (Merhavia, Israel: Sifriat Po'alim, 1961). English translation by Eugene Orenstein, Aaron Klein, and Jenny Machlowitz Klein (Philadelphia: Jewish Publication Society of America, 1985); Jay Harris, *Nachman Krochmal: Guiding the Perplexed of the Modern Age* (New York: New York University Press, 1991).

19 Rocker, *Der Sanzer Tsaddik*, 66. On R. Yechezkele, cf. A. Y. Bromberg, *The Sanzer Rav and His Dynasty*, trans. Shlomo Fox-Ashrei (Brooklyn: Mesorah Publications, 1986), 214–300.

eventually, sole owner of *Yiddishe Velt*.[20] As editor and publisher of an American daily Yiddish newspaper outside New York, Rocker could not afford the luxury of catering to exclusively one or another political or religious faction within the immigrant Jewish community, as was possible in New York. He had to be respectful to the religious and the secularist Jew alike; be sympathetic to unions while not completely disdainful of management.[21] But he also maintained his own point of view, which reflected his education and predilections. This point of view emerged even in his general articles and editorials, in which he would "draw . . . liberally on Jewish literature and folklore for illustration and proof."[22] It came out strongest in the three books he published.

The first of them, as previously mentioned, was his *Sefer Divrei Hakhamim*. Its subject was the Babylonian Talmud's interpretation of the Bible, and it was first published in 1903, near the beginning of his journalistic career. In this book, Rocker anthologized the aggadic comments scattered throughout the Babylonian Talmud on Genesis in the order of the verses, adding a commentary of his own based largely upon classic rabbinic expositions on the subject. While this book amply demonstrates the expertise in rabbinic literature Rocker had acquired in his Hungarian yeshiva education, that was not the major purpose of the book. The book rather emerged from his concern that Talmudic study, that he considered the backbone of Eastern European Jewish education, was rapidly being forgotten in the New World.[23] In his introduction, he began by speaking of the crucial importance of Talmud study in Jewish history. Then he stated:

> However now the times have changed . . . a new land and new heavens are revealed before us, and the conditions of life have changed completely. While we were dwelling on the soil of

---

20 "Samuel Rocker papers, 1910–1984 (1913–1947)," WHRS. The *Encyclopedia Judaica* indicates that Rocker began his Yiddish journalistic career in Cleveland as early as 1896.

21 He was, however, far from spineless and supported the workers in the 1911 Cloakmakers' strike even though the manufacturers threatened to withdraw their advertising. Shapiro, *Morai*, 126.

22 Gartner, *History*, 214; Shapiro, *Morai*, 127. David Eidelsberg, "Hasid un Maskil," *Jewish Morning Journal*, March 24, 1936, recalls that Rocker "sat over an editorial like over a page of Talmud, rocking back and forth."

23 Thus, the Talmud Torah, the major expression of Jewish education in North America in that era, had little room in its curriculum for Talmud. M. Ginzberg, *Keneder Adler* [Montreal], November 19, 1950; Simon Glazer, "The Talmud: Fundamental Principles," *Jewish Times* [Montreal], October 23, 1903; Seth Farber, *An American Orthodox Dreamer: Rabbi Joseph B. Soloveitchik and Boston's Maimonides School* (Hanover: University Press of New England, 2003).

Europe, even though we were occupied the entire day with making a living . . . we nonetheless devoted time to the Talmud. However, [here] we have abandoned it completely and forgotten it. . . . What has become of us here that Talmud study has become the possession of a few individuals while the nation as a whole has no part in it? I will not exaggerate if I were to say that it is habit alone . . . which is to blame in this matter. . . . It is within our power, even here, even now, to establish for ourselves at least a small period of time to study the words of the Talmud. . . . For if this present situation will continue for the period of two or three generations, then, God forbid, the teaching of the Talmud will be forgotten among us, and even more so among our descendants in our country.[24]

It is apparent that this book was not addressed to the younger, American-born generation, but rather to Rocker's contemporaries who had studied Talmud in Europe and had then abandoned it. Reading his book, Rocker hoped, would "arouse in them the memory to recall what they studied in their youth, which would arouse in them the desire . . . to establish times for Torah [study]."[25] From nostalgia for fading memories of a youthful Talmudic education, then, an improvement in the situation of American Judaism might well emerge.

The reader who peruses this book will quickly understand that Rocker was a genuine master of rabbinic literature as a whole. He will also sense that the author was definitely not interested in going much beyond traditional sources.[26] While Rocker occasionally demonstrates hesitation at accepting literally some Talmudic statements, which seem contrary to scientific observation or common sense,[27] he tends to absolve the Talmudic sages of any blame in

---

24 Rocker, *Sefer Divrei Hakhamim*, introduction, unpaginated [v].

25 Ibid., unpaginated [vi]. Rocker himself was described as having established times for personal Torah study.

26 On only two cases does he cite figures who were themselves traditionalist, but not entirely within the boundaries set by contemporary yeshivot: a citation from Moses Mendelssohn, found in the Hebrew encyclopedia *Otsar Yisrael* (ibid., 38), and one from "the sage [Alexander] Kohut" (ibid., 67). On Rocker's traditionalism and attitude toward "critical" literature, see Shapiro, *Morai*, 128–129.

27 Rocker, *Sefer Divrei Hakhamim*, 4, 17, 104.

any such misrepresentation. Thus in commenting on the Talmud's statement "Israel has no *mazal* [predestined fate],"[28] Rocker comments:

> Though in several places in the Talmud we find a belief in *mazal* . . . the sages concluded that this belief was so rooted in the heart of the masses of Israel that they were unable to uproot it completely. Truly this belief is opposed to the religion of Israel, for if we believe in *mazal*, man has no free will, God exercises no personal providence and there is no place for reward and punishment.[29]

Rocker's *Divrei Hakhamim* was thus an experiment in repositioning the "tradition" of Talmud study in the context of an American Jewish community, which by and large seemed to have relegated the necessity for Talmud study to those individuals preparing for a career in the rabbinate. Rocker's experiment apparently did not generate much enthusiasm. In his introduction, he expressed the hope that the completion of his work on Genesis would soon be followed by similar anthologies for the other books of the Pentateuch.[30] No other book in this series was published, however. In the 1920s and 1930s, Rocker would try another way of influencing his readers to preserve the Jewish tradition in their new home–by writing about the great masters of the Hasidic tradition.

In order to comprehend the novelty of what Rocker was attempting in his Hasidic works in the North American context of the early twentieth century, we have to understand the sort of "press" that Hasidism was receiving at the moment he was writing. The most authoritative reference book on Judaism at the time was the *Jewish Encyclopedia*. Searching that work for the term "hasidism" would yield the following in the entry on "Cabala": "While the doctrines of the HaBaD have shown that the Lurianic Cabala is something more than a senseless playing with letters, other forms of Hasidism, also derived from the Cabala, represent the acme of systematized cant and irrational talk."[31]

The *Jewish Encyclopedia*'s entry on "Hasidism" itself, written by Simon Dubnow (1860–1941), would inform the reader that at the beginning of the twentieth century, though the movement's "vitality cannot be doubted," it was

---

28 BT *Shabbat* 156a.
29 Rocker, *Sefer Divrei Hakhamim*, 52.
30 Ibid., unpaginated [viii].
31 S.v. "Cabala," *Jewish Encyclopedia* (New York: Funk and Wagnalls, 1901–1910), vol. 3, 470, https://www.jewishencyclopedia.com/articles/3878-cabala.

being nourished "by its stored-up reserves of spiritual power," and that "the period of stagnation which it has lately passed through must . . . result in its gradual stagnation."[32] Many reports in the Jewish press, in both English and Yiddish, treated the first manifestations of Hasidic life in North America in the late nineteenth and early twentieth centuries as if Hasidism were a disease that it were best to quarantine so as not to infect American Jewry.[33] Rocker was, therefore, going to have to counter a great deal of negativity if he was determined to present Hasidism in anything resembling a positive light.

Both his Hasidic books began as series of articles for *Yiddishe Velt*, which were afterwards published in book form, a very common method of publication of Yiddish works in North America.[34] The ostensible occasion for the first of his series of articles on Hasidism was the fiftieth anniversary of the death of Rabbi Hayyim Halberstam of Sanz in 1926.[35] Not only was Rabbi Halberstam well-known to Rocker through his personal experience, and through his father's stories,[36] but, as we will see, Rabbi Halberstam's interpretation of Hasidim, which deemphasized kabbala and miracles and stressed halakhic observance and Talmud study, was particularly congenial to Rocker.

There was, however, another reason why Rocker may have wanted to write about Rabbi Halberstam at that time. In 1916, Yitshak Even (1861–1925) had published a series of articles in the Hebrew language periodical *Ha-'Ivri* on the lengthy and bitter conflict between the Hasidism of Sanz and those

---

32 S.v. "Ḥasidim, Ḥasidism" *Jewish Encyclopedia* (New York: Funk and Wagnalls, 1901–1910), vol. 6, 255–256, https://jewishencyclopedia.com/articles/4192-chabad. Cf. Shuly Rubin Schwartz, *The Emergence of Jewish Scholarship in America: The Publication of the Jewish Encyclopedia* (Cincinnati: Hebrew Union College Press, 1991), 121. On Dubnow, see Kristi A. Groberg, "The Life and Influence of Simon Dubnov (1860–1941): An Appreciation," *Modern Judaism* 13, no. 1 (February 1993): 71–93.

33 Yosef E. Bernstein, *The Jews in Canada (in North America): An Eastern European View of the Montreal Jewish Community in 1884*, trans. Robinson (Montreal: Attic Books, 2004), 18; Ira Robinson, "The First Hasidic Rabbis in North America," *American Jewish Archives* 44 (1992): 501–515; idem, "An Identification and a Correction," *American Jewish Archives* 47 (1995): 331–332. Cf. David Rome, "The Canadian Story of Reuben Brainin, Part 2," *Canadian Jewish Archives* n.s. 48 (1996): 33–37.

34 Numerous Yiddish books in that era originated as a series of newspaper articles. An example of a series of articles, published originally in Montreal's Yiddish daily *Keneder Adler*, and subsequently appearing in book form is Hayyim Kruger, *Der Rambam: Zayn leben un Shafn* (Montreal: Keneder Adler, 1933). Cf. Rebecca Margolis, "The Yiddish Press in Montreal, 1900–1945," *Canadian Jewish Studies* 16–17 (2008–2009), 3–26.

35 Rocker, *Der Sanzer Tsaddik*, 224.

36 Ibid., introduction, unpaginated [15].

of Sadigoreh in the 1860s and 1870s, which rocked the Jewish world.[37] Even promised in his preface that his account of the conflict would be "evenhanded," favoring neither side and presenting only historical facts. In doing so, however, he also undertook to demonstrate that "all the accusations of 'new sect' [*kat hadasha*] or 'wicked sect' [*kat ha-resha'a*], which the Hasidim of Sanz called the Hasidim of Sadegureh had no substance to them."[38] In an "evenhanded" way, in other words, Even was trying to place the onus for the quarrel on the Sanzer side.[39] Though he was no longer a Sanzer Hasid in the strictest sense of the term, Rocker had retained much of his youthful loyalty to Sanz. He thus felt that he could do a better job, one fairer to Sanz than Even's account.[40] Be that as it may, it is certain that Rocker had Even's work on the conflict, as well as his other book on the Hasidic dynasty of Rabbi Israel of Rizhin in front of him.[41] Rocker learned from Even, not least, that there was an historical importance to the Hasidism of the previous generation.[42]

Rocker was also dissatisfied with attempts by the Sanzer Hasidim themselves to tell their leader's story. He thus noted in his introduction to his account of the Sanzer that:

> The history of the Sanzer Zaddik, Rabbi Ḥayyim Halberstam, has not yet been written, either in Yiddish or in the Holy Language [Hebrew]. . . . Several small books [*bikhlekh*] in the Hebrew language have indeed been written about him. They are, however, no more than a gathering together of short stories, quotations, and Torah thoughts, which have no historical value.[43]

---

37 Yitzhak Even, *Maḥloket Sanz ve-Sadigore: kol korot ha-pulmus mi-tehilato 'ad sofo, 'al pi mekorim ne'emanim uve-ruaḥ bikoret ne'emana* (New York: Ha-Yivri, 1916). On Even see "Isaac Ewen," in *Leksikon ha-Sifrut ha-Yivrit ha-Ḥadasha*, accessed February 27, 2022, https://library.osu.edu/projects/hebrew-lexicon/02806.php. It is interesting, and possibly significant, that the Artscroll account of the Sanzer dynasty chooses to dismiss this conflict in less than one page. Bromberg, *Sanzer Rav*, 128.

38 Even, *Maḥloket Sanz ve-Sadigore*, 5.

39 Ibid., 19-21.

40 Shapiro notes Rocker's attempt to be fair while yet demonstrating a certain affinity for the Sanzer side of the dispute. *Morai*, 129.

41 Yitzhak Even, *Fun'm rebin's hoyf zikhroynes un mayses gezehn, gehert un nokhdertsehlt* (New York, 1922).

42 Rocker, *Der Sanzer Tsaddik*, introduction, unpaginated.

43 Rocker, *Der Sanzer Tsaddik*, introduction, unpaginated. Rocker is probably referring to works like Raphael ha-Levi Zimetboim, *Darkhei Ḥayyim* (Cracow, 1923), reprinted in Moshkovitsh, *Kol ha-Katuv le-Ḥayyim*. On Rabbi Halberstam's halakhic influence, see Jacob

Rocker's work, by contrast, was oriented toward illuminating "a chapter of the highest importance in Jewish history."[44] In attempting to write the history of Sanzer Hasidism, Rocker was doing something that marked him as different from the mainstream of traditional, pre-modern Judaism, which did not often choose history as a favored means of literary expression.[45]

Despite the title of "history" Rocker gave to his work, the result was largely a retelling of Hasidic tales of *tsaddikim*. Rocker often prefaced these tales with some indication of the nature of the source. Thus a tale might begin "Hasidim relate," "old Hasidim relate," "Sigeter Hasidim relate," "a Hasidic legend [*aggada*] relates," or "Hasidic books state."[46] These tales were supplemented with written sources when available, as will be seen, but Rocker has been characterized by Joseph Shapiro (1902–1978) as "not delving deeply into [Hasidism's] original sources. On the contrary, Rocker himself was a "source" for the phenomenon of Hasidism."[47]

Rocker was thus by no means a "scientific" historian of Hasidism either by the standards of the Wissenschaft des Judentums, as exemplified by the publications on Hasidism and its history written by Simon Dubnow, or of the Eastern European *haskala*, as exemplified by the work of Samuel A. Horodetzky (1871–1957).[48] He was, however, well aware that there were a number of contemporary Orthodox authors who had begun to attempt to tell the Hasidic story as history and theology, and not merely to accumulate a collection of "stories, quotations, and Torah thoughts." Yitzhak Even's work, previously referred to, was one example of an author consciously writing what he considered to be Hasidic history. Another example familiar to Rocker was that of Rabbi Mattityahu Yehezkel Gutman of Husi, Romania, whose 1922 book on Rabbi Israel Ba'al Shem Tov was subtitled, in the best academic style, "His Life, His Works and His Teaching."[49] In that book, Rabbi Gutman, like Rocker, uses terms like "the

---

Katz, The "Shabbes Goy": a Study in Halakhic Flexibility (Philadelphia: Jewish Publication Society of America, 1989), 167–215 passim.

44 Rocker, Der Sanzer Tsaddik, introduction, unpaginated.

45 Yosef Hayim Yerushalmi, Zakhor: Jewish History and Jewish Memory (Seattle: University of Washington Press, 1982).

46 Rocker, Der Sanzer Tsaddik, 7, 13, 19, 26, 32; Toldos Anshei Shem, 82, 137, 151.

47 Shapiro, Morai, 128.

48 Rocker, Der Sanzer Tsaddik, 127 refers to Samuel A. Horodetsky, Ha-Hasidut veha-Hasidim (Berlin, Dvir, 1922).

49 Matityahu Yehezkel Gutman, Rabi Yisrael Ba'al Shem Tov: Hayyav, pe'ulotav ve-torato (Iaşi, 1922), cited in Rocker, Der Sanzer Tsaddik, 45, 159. The work also boasted a title page in German. Cf. Ada Rapoport-Albert, "Hagiography with Footnotes: Edifying Tales and the Writing of History in Hasidism," in Essays in Jewish Historiography, ed. Ada Rapoport-Albert

Hasidic legend" [*ha-agada ha-ḥasidit*][50] and clearly has in mind a reader who is not necessarily steeped in Hasidic life, but for whom the story of the Ba'al Shem Tov may resonate in other ways.[51]

Rocker gives us additional clues to his attitude toward Hasidism in his last book, published posthumously, in 1939, entitled *Toldot Anshei Shem*. This book consists of a collection of Rocker's publications on Rabbi Shneur Zalman of Liadi (1745–1812),[52] founder of Habad Hasidism, and the Hungarian *tsaddikim* Rabbi Yitzhak Isaac Taub (1744–1828) of Kalev, Moshe Teitelbaum (1759–1841), Yekutiel Yehuda Teitelbaum (1808–1883), Hananyah Yom Tov Lipa Teitelbaum (1836–1904), and Yeshaya Steiner known as Reb Shaya'la of Kerestir (Kerestirer, 1851–1925), also published in the *Yiddishe Velt*, apparently after his work on the *Sanzer Tsaddik*.[53] In his introductory remarks to his work on Rabbi Shneur Zalman, Rocker makes the following programmatic statement:

> Hasidic literature, stories and customs of "Good Jews,"[54] which recently have become an important part of Hebrew and Yiddish literature, have been of great use to Jewry. They have opened the curtain on a portion of the Jewish people (Hasidim), which has been portrayed by the Mitnagdim on the one hand, and the Maskilim on the other as dark and superstitious. Both the Mitnagdim and the Maskilim have noticed their mistake. Both have noticed that in that camp [of the Hasidim] there is no darkness, but rather light and life; no superstition but rather a world in which a great portion of the Jewish people found comfort and consolation, life and holiness. Whether we agree with the Hasidic way or not, we must admit that where Hasidism lived and spread its wings, Judaism remained whole, and with a soul.[55]

(Atlanta: Scholars Press, 1991), 119–159. In this article Rapoport-Albert deals almost exclusively with Habad hagiography.

50 Gutman, *Rabi Yisra'el Ba'al Shem Tov*, 32.

51 Ibid., 2.

52 This series is noteworthy in that Rabbi Shneur Zalman is the only Hasidic leader portrayed who lived other than in Galicia or Hungary. It also did not tell the entire story, stopping with Rabbi Shneur Zalman's release from Russian imprisonment on the nineteenth of Kislev 1798.

53 Rocker, *Toldos Anshei Shem*, 8. His series on Rabbi Moshe Teitelbaum apparently appeared in 1928 (79), and his essays on Rabbi Lipele Teitelbaum in 1930 (212).

54 An alternative name for *tsaddik* or rebbe, particularly in Galicia.

55 Rocker, *Toldos Anshei Shem*, 7.

Rocker clearly wanted his own writings on the Hasidim to be part of this new branch of Jewish literature and history. What was he trying to accomplish?

First and foremost, he was trying to move discourse on Hasidism within the Jewish community into the mainstream. In doing this, his strategy was two-fold. First of all, he utterly denied the accusation that the Ba'al Shem Tov, and Hasidism as a whole, did not sufficiently respect Talmudic scholarship.[56] On the contrary, the Ba'al Shem Tov is portrayed by Rocker as a great Talmudic scholar, though he admits that not all of his successors were outstanding scholars [geonim].[57] He was also prepared to admit that many later Hasidim fell short of this ideal:

> [Talmudic] learning became secondary [tafel] and Hasidism became the essential. A saying of the Rebbe became more [important] than studying a page of Talmud with Tosafot, and a "grandchild" [of the Rebbe] in swaddling clothes took on more importance than the greatest Torah scholar [gaon]. Drinking "tikkun," relating stories, conversing about "Good Jews" began playing the most important role in Hasidic life.[58]

It is worth noting, however, that if, indeed, Hasidim themselves fell short of the ideal, in Rocker's view, their leaders were hardly ever to blame. Thus in the great controversy between the Sanzer and Sadegorer Hasidim, Rocker carefully tried to minimize the active part taken by both the Sanzer and the Sadegorer leadership. In particular, Rocker took pains to distance the Sadegorer leadership from provocative acts on the Sadegoreh side such as placing the Sanzer Tsaddik in excommunication in a ceremony held at the Western Wall in Jerusalem.[59] Similarly, the persecution of Rabbi Elazar Nisan Teitelbaum by the Hasidim of Rabbi Mendele of Kassov in Sighet was described by Rocker as not emanating from Rabbi Mendele himself.[60] The Hasidic leaders, then, were almost invariably portrayed as great and benevolent Torah scholars who stood above the fray, which often pitted one Hasidic group against another.

Beyond that, Rocker put forward in his books a vision of an ideal Hasidism. This was, perhaps, not surprising for someone who, like Rocker, so

---

56 Rocker, *Der Sanzer Tsaddik*, 47.
57 Rocker, *Toldos Anshei Shem*, 148.
58 Rocker *Der Sanzer Tsaddik*, 47.
59 Ibid., 195.
60 Rocker, *Toldos Anshei Shem*, 126, 128.

closely identified with the Sanzer Tsaddik. It was a perspective that emphasized traditional Talmudic learning, and de-emphasized mysticism and claims
of miracle-working.[61] The embodiment of this ideal, of course, was Rabbi
Ḥayyim Halberstam of Sanz. Not only does Rocker portray Rabbi Halberstam
as a world-class Torah scholar [*velts gaon*] in both Talmud [*nigleh*] and kabbala [*nistar*], thus harmoniously combining "the way of the Vilna Gaon with
the way of the Ba'al Shem,"[62] but he also emphasizes the primacy of Talmud
study for Rabbi Halberstam.[63] Similarly, Rocker approves the fact that Rabbi
Halberstam and others, like Rabbi Hershele Lisker (1808–1874) discouraged
tales of miracles and wonders relating to themselves.[64] Rocker was characteris-
tically ambivalent concerning the issuing of amulets (*kameot*), which he considered a gentile custom that had been adopted by Jews during the Babylonian
exile. Rocker asserted that "many great Jewish scholars [*gedolei Yisrael*] in
nearly every generation were against the issuance of amulets, and that those
rabbis who issued them, like Rabbi Jonathan Eybeschutz (1690–1764), were
persecuted for it. Therefore, even Hasidic rebbes, for the most part, dispensed
amulets in secret."[65]

The Hasidic world that Rocker portrayed in his books was one in which
modern Jews, who had abandoned the Hasidic tradition, yet derived many
positive things. Thus, for example, "modern" cantors came to Hasidic singers
for inspiration, and Rabbi Isaac Kalever's songs were sung by even the "enlight-
ened" among Hungarian Jewry.[66] At least some non-observant Jews came to
Hasidic rabbis for their blessing.[67] In a word, the Hasidism he portrayed was
one in which those elements that would appear most foreign to modern civilization were either suppressed or else de-emphasized. One of the most important aspects of this suppression is that in his lengthy portrait of Rabbi Hayyim
Halberstam and his teachings, he barely refers to his rulings that forbade
Jews, especially women, from adopting Western modes of dress.[68] The major
exception to this, which Rocker could hardly have avoided, had to do with the

---

61 Rocker, *Der Sanzer Tsaddik*, 79.
62 Ibid., 42.
63 Ibid., 47; Hayyim Halberstam, *She'elot u-Teshuvot Divrei Ḥayyim* (Lvov, 1875), part 2, no.
    47, 33.
64 Rocker, *Toldos Anshei Shem*, 200.
65 Ibid., 109–110.
66 Rocker, *Der Sanzer Tsaddik*, 35–36, 39. Rocker notes that Rabbi Halberstam would not let
    "modern" cantors perform for him.
67 Rocker, *Toldos Anshei Shem*, 182–183.
68 Halberstam, *She'elot u-Teshuvot Divrei Ḥayyim*, part 1, no. 30, 54–55.

notorious accusation that the women of the Sadegoreh dynasty had adopted western dress and manners.[69]

A second factor to note is Rocker's treatment of Maskilim. They were, as mentioned earlier, depicted as mistaken opponents of Hasidism, like the Mitnagdim. They are generally portrayed in Rocker's books entirely from a Hasidic perspective. Thus a Maskil of Chernovits, Dr. Yehuda Leib Reitman, who figured in the affair of Rabbi Dov (Berenyu) of Leova, which touched off the Sanz-Sadegoreh conflict, is described as follows: "He was an early Maskil and a student of Joseph Perl (1773–1839), the author of *Megale Tmirin*. [He was] a terrible 'devourer' of Hasidim [*Hasidim fresser*] and a known nonbeliever [*apikoros*]."[70] There is nothing in his books that overtly lets the reader in on the fact that Rocker was in fact greatly influenced by the works of Galician Maskilim such as Joseph Perl, Nahman Krochmal (1785–1840), and Shlomo Yehuda Rapoport (1790–1867).[71]

What, then, was Rocker trying to do by writing his Hasidic books in Yiddish in Cleveland, Ohio? Perhaps the best answer is to compare Rocker's books with one written at the same period by the editor of Montreal's Yiddish daily, *Der Keneder Adler*, Hirsch Wolofsky.[72] Its title was *Oyf Eybiken Kvall: Gedanken un batrachtungen fun dem hayntigen idishen leben un shtreben, in likht fun unzer alter un eybig-nayer tora, eingeteylt loyt di parshiyos fun der vokh* (*From the Eternal Source: Thoughts and observations from contemporary Jewish life and aspirations in the light of our old and eternally new Torah, organized according to the weekly [Torah] portions*).[73] As with Rocker's books, Wolofsky first published his book as a series of articles in his newspaper in 1928–1929. He was attempting to create nothing less than a contemporary commentary or homily (*drush*) on the Pentateuch. The form the book took, commentary, as well as its division according to the weekly synagogue Torah readings, reflected a respect for and an appreciation of the Judaic tradition. Wolofsky appropriated that tradition

---

69 Rocker, *Der Sanzer Tsaddik*, 140, 154. It is instructive to contrast this treatment with Even's emphasis on this importance of this charge. Even, *Mahloket Sanz ve-Sadigore*, 8, 13.

70 Rocker, *Der Sanzer Tsaddik*, 158.

71 Shapiro, *Morai*, 124.

72 On Hirsch Wolofsky, see his autobiography *Mayn Lebens Rayze* (Montreal: Keneder Adler, 1946). This memoir was translated into English as *The Journey of My Life* (Montreal: Keneder Adler, 1945), and into French as *Mayn Lebens Rayze: Un demi-siècle de vie yiddish à Montréal*, trans. Pierre Anctil (Sillery: Septentrion, 2000). Cf. also Robinson, *Rabbis and Their Community*, chapter 8.

73 Hirsch Wolofsky, *Oyf Eybiken Kvall: Gedanken un batrachtungen fun dem hayntishen yiddishen leben un shtreben, in likht fun unzer alter un eybig-nayer tora, eingeteylt loyt di parshiyos fun der vokh* (Montreal: Keneder Adler, 1930).

in order to shed new light on the dynamics of the contemporary Jewish community, whose life and aspirations Wolofsky wished to reflect. In his introduction, Wolofsky began by consciously placing his work within the tradition of the ancient midrashic and later homiletic (*drush*) literature of Judaism. These premodern works, Wolofsky asserted, sought to explain contemporary problems in terms of the Torah, utilizing the literary means of allegory, fantasy and imagination. These elements were added to the true story of Torah[74] in order to affect the hearts of the audience. This process was precisely what Wolofsky wished to imitate, only in the twentieth century and "according to the American version [*nusakh*]."[75] In the North American Jewish cultural atmosphere, *drush* also had to become different. There was no twentieth-century audience for homilies lasting hours on end. Jews who were willing to listen at all to words of Torah wanted the speaker to come to the point in fifteen to twenty minutes without either elaborate introductions or difficult questions. Having this situation in mind, Wolofsky was not about to create a "serious" commentary on the Torah in the old style.[76] Wolofsky, in writing this work, thought of his enterprise in the context of the age-old Jewish custom of reviewing the weekly Torah portion (*ma'avir sedra zayn*) with the original biblical text read twice and the translation/interpretation (*targum*) once. At present, however, Wolofsky asserted that the original "text" of Jewish life has largely been forgotten and that therefore contemporary Jews are living their lives at a remove from the original (*targum-lebn*) in a world where practically nothing is "original" and all is *targum*. For Jews living in such a world, Wolofsky proposed in his book to present a series of homilies, which might, indeed, be more *targum* than original, but which were conceived by him to be in the spirit of the original.[77]

I would say that Rocker, like Wolofsky, understood that the immigrant Jews who constituted his audience had mostly detached themselves from an immediate connection with the Jewish tradition of yesteryear, but might yet be reached through an innovative literature emanating from that tradition. Wolofsky found himself in the mainstream of a cohort of creative Yiddish-speaking contemporaries in Montreal, who, through their teaching and publications, attempted to utilize the hallowed resources of the Jewish past, including

---

74 It is clear from a careful reading of *Eybigen Kvall* that Wolofsky believed in the essential historicity of the narratives of the Torah.

75 Wolofsky, *Oyf Eybiken Kvall*, 2, 5. It is worth noting that, for the most part, Wolofsky speaks of "America," and does not seem to be looking at a Canadian specificity in the situations he depicts.

76 Ibid., 6.

77 Ibid., 7.

Midrash, and Mishna, to recreate a thriving and culturally innovative Jewish community through the medium of Yiddish. As David Roskies described this phenomenon, the writers took for granted that the old, Judaic culture of Eastern Europe had to be reinvented. If the original had become inaccessible to the average Jew in the street, then a compelling Jewish life in *targum* had to be established both intellectually and institutionally.[78]

Rocker himself had a somewhat similar group of intellectual companions in Cleveland. They included pioneering Hebrew educator H. A. Friedland.[79] More importantly, however, they included a pair of Orthodox rabbis who originated in Galicia and Hungary, respectively, and who themselves were authors of books about Hasidism, which constituted departures from traditional Hasidic literature, yet which retained a respect for both Hasidism and Orthodox Judaism. One was Menachem Mendel Eckstein, rabbi of Congregation Bnai Jacob Anshei Marmorosh of Cleveland, author of *Tena'e ha-Nefesh le-Hassagat ha-Hasidut* (1920/1).[80] The other was Rabbi Yekutiel Greenwald (1889–1955) of Columbus, Ohio, whose monumental oeuvre includes books on the Jews of Hungary,[81] and several biographies of great rabbis.[82] Rabbis Eckstein and Greenwald are credited by Rocker with lending him books and sharing with him their knowledge of Hasidism.[83] An intensive study of these works would doubtless yield more insight into Rocker's intellectual world.

When Samuel Rocker died in 1936, his funeral service, as reported by the *New York Times* was conducted by rabbis of the three branches of American Judaism: Reform, Conservative, and Orthodox.[84] It is nonetheless clear that characterizing Rocker on the standard Orthodox-Conservative-Reform continuum of twentieth-century American Jewry does a disservice to the complexity of his personality. A better basis of understanding was presented by three of

---

78 David Roskies, "Yiddish in Montreal: the Utopian Experiment," in *An Everyday Miracle: Yiddish Culture in Montreal*, ed. Ira Robinson et al. (Montreal: Vehicule Press, 1990), 22–38.

79 Rocker, *Toldos Anshei Shem*, 5. On Friedland, see Sylvia F. Abrams and Lifsa Schacter, "Abraham Hayyim Firedland and the Context, Structures, and Content of Jewish Education," in *Cleveland Jews and the Making of a Midwestern Community*, ed. Sean Martin and John J. Grabowski (New Brunswick: Rutgers UnIversity Press, 2020), 58–79.

80 This book was later reprinted in Israel under another title: Menachem Mendel Eckstein, *Mavo' le-Torat ha-Hasidut* (Tel-Aviv: Netsah, 1960).

81 Yekutiel Greenwald, *Ha-Yehudim be-Ungaria* (Vac, 1912); idem, *Le-Pelagot Yisrael be-Ungaria* (Devo, Romania, 1929); idem, *Toizend Yohr Yiddish Leben in Ungarn* (New York, 1945).

82 Greenwald, *Ha-Rav R. Yehonatan Eybeshits* (New York: Hadar Linotyping, 1954).

83 Rocker, *Toldos Anshei Shem*, 160, 215.

84 *New York Times*, March 19, 1936, 25.

his contemporaries who wrote about him in the language in which he wrote–
Yiddish. Baruch Zuckerman, an important leader of the Po'alei Zion movement
in the first half of the twentieth century, compared Rocker in his memoirs to
Hillel Zeitlin (1871–1942), the Warsaw journalist and mystic who, in the words
of Arthur Green, "tried to create chasidism for those who lived outside the chasidic world."[85]

The Yiddish journalist David Eidelsberg wrote an obituary for Rocker in
the *Jewish Morning Journal* (*Morgen Journal*) of New York on March 24, 1936
under the title "Hasid and Maskil" (*Hasid un Maskil*). Rocker, in Eidelsberg's
opinion:

> ... embodied the infrequent combination of Hasid and Maskil–
> first of all Hasid, and then Maskil. ... In his youth, like many
> Torah students of that era, he was satiated with the rationalistic
> teachings [*torah*] of the Haskala, but his Hasidic soul was not
> touched. So to speak, he ate the fruit and threw away the peel. In
> his best maskilic convictions, he remained a Hasid ...

> Rocker used to say that great Maskilim like [Joseph] Perl, [Isaac
> Baer] Levinsohn (1788–1860), [Isaac] Erter (1791–1851), and
> [Nahman] Krochmal persecuted Hasidism to the end because
> they were completely Jews of mind, while a deeper [maskilic]
> thinker like Eliezer Zweifel (1815–1888)[86] looked on Jewry
> also with the eyes of the heart. And thus, as a Maskil he was able
> to evaluate the great importance of the Hasidic movement for
> Jewish history. Rocker did not only write well about Hasidism,
> but he practised its high morality and life.[87]

Joseph Shapiro, who had worked closely with Rocker for several years on the
staff of *Yiddishe Velt*, and had subsequently moved to Palestine, also wrote of
Rocker's paradoxical mixture of Hasid and Maskil:

> Reb Joshua Rocker, the Torah scholar [*talmid hokhom*] with
> the clear mind, was educated in a Hasidic environment and was

---

85 Cited in Shapiro, *Morai*, 133. Cf. John Dorfman, "Radical Theology: Arthur Green Translates
   a Chasidic Classic," *Forward*, December 4, 1998.
86 *Encyclopedia Judaica*, vol. 16, cols. 1245–1246.
87 Eidelsberg, "Hasid un Maskil."

well versed [*baki*] in its teaching . . . when he distanced himself from it, like Rabbi Meir, he ate the content and threw away the husk. . . .

Often I felt as if I were sitting in front of one of the most faithful heirs of ...the generation of true *maskilim*: an heir in knowledge, humor, love of Israel, and also an heir in the struggle against those who sought to bring foreign culture into Jewish life. . . . The struggle of Joshua Rocker against assimilation in all its forms was conducted with enthusiasm, and the entire fervor of his Jewish soul.[88]

In his struggle to create a viable contemporary Judaism, Joshua Rocker attempted to use the power of the Hasidic tradition, not to oppose modernization as such, but to show his readers that there were different paths available to them as Jews other than a lockstep acculturation into an American "melting pot." By portraying the leaders of nineteenth-century Hasidism positively in the way he did, he sought to convince his readers that the ideas and ideals of the Hasidic tradition had continued relevance in the here and now, and had not simply left been behind in the forward march of civilization.[89] For Joshua Rocker, there was something in Hasidism and its story that could speak to his contemporaries, and help them as they engaged in the vital balancing act between the Judaic tradition and Western civilization that characterized all varieties of modern Judaism.

---

88 Yosef Shapiro, "Reb Yehoshua Rocker," JW, May 4, 1936.
89 Robinson, "Hasidic Hagiography," 409.

CHAPTER 4

A "Jewish Monkey Trial": The Cleveland Jewish Center and the Emerging Borderline between Orthodox and Conservative Judaism in 1920s North America[1]

In the 1920s the world of Orthodox Judaism in North America felt itself besieged on many sides.[2] In particular, it was shaken by a movement within the rank and file of many Orthodox synagogues, influenced by a growing cohort of English-speaking rabbis educated at the Jewish Theological Seminary of America in New York.[3] This movement challenged traditional synagogues to

---

1   A French-language version of this chapter was published as "La formation d'une identité juive américaine: L'émergence du judaïsme 'conservateur' et 'orthodoxe' dans les années 1920," *Théologiques* 24, no. 2 (2016): 121–146.

2   For an interesting and insightful contemporary global analysis of Orthodox Judaism in America, see Gedaliah Bublick, *Der Sakhakl in Amerikaner Yyidntum* (New York, 1927), which originated as a series of articles in New York's Orthodox-oriented Yiddish daily, *Tageblatt*. On Orthodoxy in America, see Jeffrey Gurock, *Orthodox Jews in America* (Bloomington: Indiana University Press, 2009); Jonathan Sarna, *American Judaism* (New Haven: Yale University Press, 2004); Aaron Rakeffet-Rothkoff, *The Silver Era in American Jewish Orthodoxy* (New York: Yeshiva University Press, 1981).

3   On the Jewish Theological Seminary and its graduates in this period, see Michael Cohen, *The Birth of Conservative Judaism: Solomon Schechter's Disciples and the Creation of an American Religious Movement* (New York: Columbia University Press, 2012). Cf. Ira Robinson, "Cyrus Adler: President of the Jewish Theological Seminary, 1915–1940," in *Tradition Renewed: A History of the Jewish Theological Seminary*, ed. Jack Wertheimer (New York: Jewish Theological Seminary Press, 1997), vol. 1, 103–159.

"modernize" themselves by abolishing the separate seating of men and women in their sanctuaries. Proponents of such changes often argued forcefully that doing so would not necessarily mean relinquishing the definition of such a synagogue as "Orthodox."[4] The resulting conflict between supporters and opponents of this form of synagogue liberalization helped to define a growing divergence between "Conservative" and "Orthodox" Judaism in North America.

This article will analyze one of the most prominent cases of "Orthodox" synagogues' adopting mixed seating—that of the Jewish Center of Cleveland, Ohio. Under the leadership of its Jewish Theological Seminary-trained Rabbi Solomon Goldman,[5] The Jewish Center adopted mixed seating in 1925. Rabbi Goldman's arguments for mixed seating, as we will see, succeeded in winning over a majority of the congregation to his views. However, as elsewhere, the dissenting minority within the congregation refused to concede the principle that their synagogue, founded for the perpetuation of "Orthodox Judaism," had the right to do this and brought their case to court. The case was before the courts for several years in Cleveland's Court of Common Pleas, two courts of appeals, and the Supreme Court of Ohio. It attracted local, national, and international publicity and helped to define what Orthodox and Conservative Judaism in North America represented for an entire generation.

Historians of Orthodoxy and Conservatism in America are aware of this case and its importance and have cited it in their respective analyses.[6] This article reviews sources available to previous researchers. However, it also brings to bear extensive archival documentation currently located in Cleveland Heights, Ohio, which had been preserved by the family of one of the prime instigators of the lawsuit, Abraham A. Katz. This material sheds new light on the case and

---

4   On this issue, see Jonathan Sarna, "The Debate over Mixed Seating in the American Synagogue," in *The American Synagogue: A Sanctuary Transformed*, ed. Jack Wertheimer (New York: Cambridge University Press, 1987), 363–394. Cf. also idem, "Seating and the American Synagogue," in *Belief and Behavior: Essays in the New Religious History*, ed. Philip Vandermeer and Robert P. Swierenga (New Brunswick: Rutgers University Press, 1991), 189–206. From an Orthodox perspective see Baruch Litwin, ed., *The Sanctity of the Synagogue* (New York: Spero Foundation, 1959).

5   On Goldman, see Jacob J. Weinstein, *Solomon Goldman: A Rabbi's Rabbi* (New York: Ktav, 1973).

6   On the gradual separation between Orthodox and Conservative Judaism see Sarna, *American Judaism*, 193. For mentions of the Cleveland case, see Sarna, "The Debate over Mixed Seating," 392, n. 73; Gurock, *Orthodox Jews in America*, 159–160; Cohen, *The Birth of Conservative Judaism*, 86–88; Alan Brill, "The Orthodox–Conservative Split and Rabbi Solomon Goldman," accessed 26 October 2015, https://kavvanah.wordpress.com/2013/11/09/the-orthodox-conservative-split-and-rabbi-solomon-goldman.

its consequences, particularly from the perspective of the dissident Orthodox minority. It also, importantly, contains the complete transcript of the expert testimony of some of the most prominent American Orthodox leaders of the era, whose testimony and cross-examination by Goldman yields much information of importance.

The Jewish Community of Cleveland in the Early Twentieth Century

In the early decades of the twentieth century, the Jewish community of Cleveland constituted one of the largest concentrations of Jewish population in the United States.[7] Among the numerous synagogues that existed in Cleveland in this period were large and influential Reform temples, which had themselves begun as traditionalist congregations,[8] as well as a number of generally smaller Eastern European congregations that identified themselves as "Orthodox." However, the term "Orthodox" in North America in those decades was anything but sharply defined, other than in opposition to Reform. Orthodox congregations in early twentieth-century Cleveland followed patterns common in most North American centers of Jewish population. Congregations tended to form on the basis of common place of origin or liturgy.[9] Many if not most of these synagogues tolerated members who were no longer strict observers of the Sabbath because of the overwhelming economic realities they faced in North America.[10] On the other hand, some Cleveland synagogues tried to resist these

---

7   On the history of the Jews of Cleveland, see Gartner, *History of the Jews of Cleveland*. Cf. also Vincent and Rubenstein, *Merging Traditions*; and Wertheim and Bennett, *Remembering: Cleveland's Jewish Voices*. Also useful is Wiesenfeld, *Jewish Life in Cleveland*. Cf. also Robinson, "'A Link in the Great American Chain," 14–34.

8   Sarna, "The Debate over Mixed Seating," 372.

9   Gartner, *History of the Jews of Cleveland*, 177. Cf. Ira Robinson, "Anshe Sfard: the Creation of the First Hasidic Congregations in North America," *American Jewish Archives* 57 (2005): 53–66.

10 One of the key issues facing motivated Orthodox Jews was finding jobs that did not involve working on the Sabbath. Organizations such as Cleveland's Jewish Sabbath Association were founded to help. Brudno's cigar factory, which was owned by an Orthodox Jew and which did not require work on Sabbaths and holidays, thus attracted, among others, "a few young men who were ordained rabbis and some 'genteel' young men who in the old country had never done a lick of work." These Orthodox men, "dignified, pious Jews with handsome beards," in Joseph Morgenstern's description, sat at one table and discussed Torah. This was a discussion in which Brudno, the owner, would "often" take part. Brudno is described by Rose Pastor as "a picturesque patriarch with his long black beard and his

pressures. Members of Cleveland's Synagogue of the Government of Grodno thus pledged to strictly refrain from labor on Saturdays and Jewish holidays,[11] and the Hungarian Congregation Shomre Shabbos accepted only Sabbath-observant members.[12] Yet another cause of the proliferation of synagogues was strife within congregations, one major cause of which was the issue of separate seating of men and women. This issue arose in Cleveland's Congregation Bnai Jeshurun in 1904. The adoption of mixed seating by Bnai Jeshurun led to the founding of an Orthodox breakaway congregation, Oheb Zedek.[13] A similar controversy, albeit much more consequential, was that of the Jewish Center.

The Jewish Center of Cleveland

The Jewish Center was formed as the result of a 1917 merger between congregations Anshe Emeth and Beth Tefilo. Anshe Emeth had been founded in 1869 by immigrants from Poland. Its leadership soon began to discuss issues that would in the end lead it away from Orthodoxy. Thus, members of Anshe Emeth debated the issue of mixed seating as early as the late 1880s, undoubtedly under the influence of Cleveland's dominant Reform temples. At that time, however, they did not make any changes. There were also congregational debates in the nineteenth century over the continuance of the priestly blessing (*dukhaning*) as well as on the elimination of public announcements of donations at the time of the Torah reading (*shenodering*); these changes were not made at that time, either. When the synagogue moved to new quarters in 1903, it did not maintain the traditional central platform (*bimah*) for Torah reading. This innovation caused the resignation of "some of the [synagogue's] very pious members."[14]

---

tall black skull-cap. . . . In this godless America he would give them plenty of work in a shop where the Sabbath was kept holy. It was his strength, for they would work in no shop where the Sabbath was not kept holy." Morgenstern, *I Have Considered My Days*, 113–114; Wertheim and Bennett, *Remembering: Cleveland's Jewish Voices*, 87.

11 Gartner, *History of the Jews of Cleveland*, 133, 177.

12 "Shomre Shabbos," Jewish Cleveland, accessed February 17, 2015, http://jewishcleveland. weebly.com/shomre-shabbos.html (link no longer active). The website of the congregation indicates the founding date of 1904: Shomre Shabbos, accessed October 14, 2022, https:// shomreshabbos.com/. Lloyd Gartner presents a founding date of 1906: *History of the Jews of Cleveland*, 177.

13 Gartner, *History of the Jews of Cleveland*, 168–169.

14 See Park Synagogue website, accessed April 2015, http://www.parksynagogue.org.

Anshe Emeth accepted Samuel Margolies as its rabbi in 1904.[15] Margolies came to Cleveland with a unique preparation for the American rabbinate. He was the son of one of the most prominent immigrant Orthodox rabbis in America, Moses Sebulun Margolies (Ramaz).[16] Samuel's family sent him to Eastern Europe for advanced rabbinic training at the Telz Yeshiva. When he returned to America, he entered Harvard College and graduated in 1902. He thus came to Cleveland with the ability to preach and interact with his congregants in English as well as Yiddish. As the first English-speaking Orthodox rabbinic spokesman in Cleveland,[17] Margolies took on a leadership role in a number of initiatives designed to unite the Eastern European immigrant community in Cleveland. These included the Union of Jewish Organizations (1906–1909),[18] an attempt to organize a Cleveland branch of the Union of Orthodox Jewish Congregations of America (1913),[19] and the Cleveland Kehilla (1913–1914).[20]

Margolies was different in several respects from his colleagues in the Orthodox rabbinate of Cleveland. He was, for instance, clean-shaven—an important sartorial statement in an era in which Orthodox rabbis were almost by definition bearded and in which achieving a clean-shaven look meant either utilizing a razor, forbidden by Judaic law (halakhah), or else applying a chemical depilatory powder. Margolies also introduced confirmation and late Friday night services to the congregation, in clear imitation of the practices of Reform temples. Confirmation at least was adopted by other Cleveland Orthodox congregations of this era as well.[21] Margolies was also a founder of the Cleveland

---

15 "Margolies, Samuel," ECH, accessed February 12, 2015, http://ech.case.edu/cgi/article. pl?id=MS9.
16 "Rabbi Margolies Dies of Pneumonia; Dean of Orthodox Synagogue Heads, 85, Zionist Leader and Jewish Educator. Founder of Relief Group Rose from Sickbed in 1933 to Address Meeting of Protest Against Anti-Semitism," *New York Times*, August 26, 1936. Cf. Adam S. Ferziger, *Beyond Sectarianism: The Realignment of American Orthodox Judaism* (Detroit: Wayne State University Press, 2015), 44–45.
17 Gartner, *History of the Jews of Cleveland*, 172.
18 "Union of Jewish Organizations," ECH, accessed February 12, 2015 http://ech.case.edu/ cgi/article.pl?id=UOJO.
19 JW, July 25, 1913, 4.
20 "Kehillah," ECH, accessed February 15, 2015, http://ech.case.edu/cgi/article.pl?id=K2. Cf. David Kaufman, *Shul with a Pool: The "Synagogue-Center" in American Jewish History* (Hanover, NH: University Press of New England, 1999), 226.
21 For a picture of Margolies with the Anshe Emeth confirmation class of 1913, see Vincent and Rubenstein, *Merging Traditions*, 73. A program from the Oheb Zedek confirmation program of 1937 is preserved in KFA. For confirmation ceremonies and late Friday night services in an Orthodox synagogue in Columbus, Ohio, see Ferziger, *Beyond Sectarianism*, 32.

Hebrew School, which was ideologically opposed by some members of the Cleveland Orthodox rabbinate for its modernist tendencies.[22]

One of Margolies's initiatives was his encouragement of the founding of Congregation Beth Tefilo in the Glenville neighborhood in 1912 and its 1917 merger with Anshe Emeth.[23] Shortly after the merger, Margolies died in an automobile accident, and the merged congregation did not acquire a new rabbi until 1919, when it hired Samuel Benjamin, a recent graduate of the Jewish Theological Seminary. Benjamin presided over a congregation that continued Margolies's innovations of late Friday night services and confirmation.[24] Benjamin's three-year tenure as rabbi was marked by the successful effort of the newly merged Anshe Emeth–Beth Tefilo to build a magnificent Jewish Center with a large auditorium, spacious classrooms for the Hebrew school, and up-to-date sports facilities on East 105th Street, the emerging center of the Cleveland Jewish community.[25] The construction reportedly cost the then-astronomical sum of $1 million. However, Rabbi Benjamin, who worked very hard to make the Jewish Center a reality, was not destined to dedicate it. In 1922 Benjamin was suddenly ousted from his position as rabbi and replaced by another Jewish Theological Seminary graduate, Solomon Goldman, who had served for the previous four years as rabbi of Cleveland's Bnai Jeshurun congregation. The issue that got Benjamin fired, according to journalist Leon Wiesenfeld, was that Benjamin "stood with the Orthodox group in the synagogue and was ousted by those in the congregation who wanted liberal reforms who replaced him with Rabbi Solomon Goldman."[26]

But what liberal reforms did Benjamin oppose? There is no record of his opposition to the congregation's previous innovations of no central *bimah*, late Friday night services, and confirmation. The overriding issue that found him in opposition to the "liberal" elements of the congregation was that of mixed seating. In a letter to Abraham A. Katz, the leader of the congregation's "Orthodox" faction, Benjamin stated that the question of mixed seating had been the subject of "serious discussion" in the congregation during his rabbinate. At the request of the Jewish Center board, Benjamin traveled to New York to consult

---

22 On the tensions between American "Talmud Torahs" and Orthodoxy, see Bublick, *Der Sakhakl in Amerikaner Yidntum*, 123ff.

23 The merger took effect on January 1, 1917. A protest resolution is preserved in KFA. Cf. "Margolies, Samuel."

24 Jacob Heller to Abraham Katz, 26 Elul 5689, 1 October 1929, 2, KFA.

25 On the Jewish Center movement, see Kaufman, *Shul with a Pool*. Cf. Bublick, *Der Sakhakl in Amerikaner Yidntum*, 32, 65, 78.

26 Wiesenfeld, *Jewish Life in Cleveland*, 70.

the faculty of the Jewish Theological Seminary, including Talmud Professor Louis Ginzberg (1873–1953) and President Cyrus Adler (1863–1940), both of whom were opposed to mixed seating. Adler told him that that he was "bitterly opposed to mixed and promiscuous seating and would sooner consent to an organ in the synagogue."[27] Adler's stance, which Rabbi Benjamin evidently adopted as his own, sealed Benjamin's fate at the Jewish Center.

The Jewish Center and the Future of Cleveland Jewry

For both sides of the dispute over mixed seating at the Jewish Center, the stakes were high. In a 1925 letter to Rabbi Herbert Goldstein (1890–1970), president of the Union of Orthodox Jewish Congregations of America,[28] Abraham Katz expressed what he felt was at stake:

> The Jewish Center of Cleveland is the only institution in our city having facilities, drawing to itself the younger generation of Orthodox Jews. . . . The other [Orthodox] congregations are small in comparison . . . and the young men and women have nowhere else to go.[29]

Jacob D. Goldman, one of Katz's liberal opponents, could not have agreed with him more on this point: "I do not know of any single institution in the country that can justly claim for itself the esteem, prestige, and influence that the Center holds in the Jewish community of Cleveland."[30] Both sides, then, were fighting for their vision of the future of Cleveland Jewry.

Katz recalled that, as a boy, he and his father[31] "came together in a little Shul to pray and my friends attended temples decorated beautifully." He asked

---

27 Samuel Benjamin to Abraham Katz, n.d. (marked received 1 December 1927), KFA.
28 On Goldstein, see Aaron I. Reichel, *The Maverick Rabbi: Rabbi Herbert S. Goldstein and the Institutional Synagogue—A New Organizational Form* (Norfolk, VA: Donning, 1984).
29 Abraham Katz to Herbert Goldstein, April 27, 1925, KFA.
30 Jacob D. Goldman, letter to editor, *Jewish Advocate* [Boston], December 22, 1927, KFA.
31 His father, Joseph Katz, who died in 1925 at age seventy-five, was described in an obituary as immigrating to Cleveland in 1881 from Lithuania, having studied in "various European yeshivot." He was described as "a Talmudist of note and a rigid adherent of Talmudical Judaism." In the Orthodox community of Cleveland, "there was not a movement . . . pertaining to traditional Judaism and learning for the past forty years in which . . . [he] was not one of the leading workers or advisors." "Joseph Katz Dies in Palestine," n.d., KFA.

his father, "Why can't we have such beautiful temples to pray in?"[32] The Jewish Center was in so many ways the answer to his prayers. With it, Orthodox Jews in Cleveland would not have to feel inferior to Reform Jews.

Katz envisioned the Jewish Center as "a modern Orthodox congregation, standing for traditional Judaism." Its Orthodoxy, in his mind, was not affected by either the training of its rabbi at the Jewish Theological Seminary or its affiliation with the seminary-oriented United Synagogue of America. For him the affiliation was "for the purpose of strengthening our traditional Judaism."[33] Like many other Orthodox Jews of this era, Katz was not really fazed by the label "Conservative." He had thought of Conservative Judaism as "Orthodox Judaism slightly modernized."[34] Katz, in a 1927 letter to Goldstein, asserted that the contract consolidating the two congregations, Anshe Emeth and Beth Tefilo, which took effect on 1 January 1917, used the term "Traditional Judaism," while the Jewish Center constitution, adopted shortly after the consolidation, used the term "Orthodox." As Katz remarked, "To us the terms were similar."[35]

Katz's detractors alleged that his motivation in his opposition was something other than altruistic zealousness for Orthodox Judaism. Rabbi Goldman expressed this view:

> Mr. A. A. Katz has . . . occupied the office of secretary in the Cleveland Jewish Center under the spiritual leadership of Rabbi Goldman and was known to be one of his staunchest admirers. It was only upon being defeated several years ago, and after losing his office as secretary, that Mr. Katz suddenly began to find fault with Rabbi Goldman's conception of Judaism.[36]

This view of Katz was essentially reiterated by Jacob Heller, a staunchly Orthodox Jew:

> Your Centre was (and is) a stalwart member of the "United Synagogue," united to destroy Judaism. I fail to recall that you or anyone else protested at the time against these things. When

---

32 Abraham A. Katz, draft speech to the Union of Orthodox Jewish Congregations of America, 7, KFA.
33 Abraham Katz to Elias Solomon, September 15, 1925, KFA.
34 Abraham Katz to Leon Spitz, August 3, 1925, KFA.
35 Abraham Katz to Goldstein, May 17, 1927, KFA.
36 Jacob D. Goldman, letter to editor, *Jewish Advocate* [Boston], December 22, 1927, KFA.

Goldman was taken, you knew that he came from Bnai Jeshurun, you knew that he was openly a Reformer, yet I fail to recall that anyone protested.[37]

Indeed, there is no record of a protest by Katz in a Jewish Center board meeting either at the hiring of Rabbi Goldman or even at the possibility, discussed by the board, of merging with Congregation Bnai Jeshurun, which already had mixed seating.[38]

The Transformation of the Jewish Center

Katz's vision of a "Modern Orthodox" Jewish Center was to be thwarted by the accession of Goldman as the center's rabbi. Rabbi Goldman strongly believed in mixed seating as the best way to maintain the essential continuity of traditional Judaism in America. From 1918 to 1922, he had been the rabbi of Bnai Jeshurun in Cleveland, which had adopted mixed seating. Many of those who voted to hire Rabbi Goldman saw an opportunity to make the Jewish Center into a truly shining example of modern, traditional Judaism in Cleveland and beyond, and chose him clearly expecting that he would introduce mixed seating.

It was soon apparent, however, that Rabbi Goldman would have opposition within the congregation for the changes he wished to make. On August 24, 1922, shortly after he had become the Jewish Center's rabbi and just a few weeks before the High Holidays, a congregational board meeting was held at which Rabbi Goldman spoke in favor of mixed seating. With the considerable eloquence and learning he possessed, Goldman attempted to reassure the board that the change he recommended was legitimate from a Jewish perspective. He contended that there was no law in the halakhic code specifically forbidding the practice. He also argued that there were many other laws that Orthodox Jews regularly violate as a matter of necessity under American conditions that are as important as or perhaps even more important than the issue of mixed seating in the synagogue.

At that meeting, seven people spoke in favor of mixed seating and thirteen—led by Katz, who was at that time the congregation's secretary—spoke

---

37 Jacob Heller to Abraham Katz, 26 Elul 5689 [October 1, 1929], 2, KFA.
38 Jewish Center board of directors minutes, KFA.

against it. Seeing that his mixed-seating proposal would not pass, Goldman suggested a compromise in which a section of the balcony be reserved for mixed seating. Katz claimed that had it not been for his opposition, Rabbi Goldman would have had his way then and there and that he personally thwarted an attempt to sell mix-seating tickets also in a lower-level section.[39] According to the account of Samuel J. Bialosky (1874–1935), a Goldman supporter and subsequently president of the congregation, during the High Holidays of 1922 the mixed-seating balcony was "packed to suffocation and the [men only] main floor two-thirds empty."[40]

At this point Rabbi Goldman still identified himself and was generally recognized in the community as Orthodox.[41] Nonetheless, his liberal tendencies were becoming more and more apparent. At the formal dedication of the Jewish Center building, on October 22, 1922, it is significant that the Orthodox rabbis present—Benjamin Gittelsohn, Ozer Paley, and Zachariah Sachs—were given essentially ceremonial tasks, including reciting the opening prayer and placing the Torah scrolls in the ark. Meanwhile, the substantive rabbinical addresses, other than Goldman's, were given by the two most prominent Reform rabbis in Cleveland, Louis Wolsey (1877–1953) and Abba Hillel Silver (1893–1963).[42]

In response to the threat of momentous change at the Jewish Center, Abraham Katz led the Orthodox elements in the congregation to fight what they regarded as a betrayal of Orthodox Judaism. One of the means they utilized in their fight was to convert the newspaper *Der Yiddisher Waechter* (Jewish Guardian), under the editorial guidance of Benjamin, to an anti-Goldman organ. Thus, according to journalist Leon Wiesenfeld, "the purpose of the new publication was . . . to fight Rabbi Solomon Goldman and the Jewish Center."[43]

---

39 Abraham Katz to Leon Spitz, August 3, 1925, KFA.

40 Samuel J. Bialosky, "The Cleveland Jewish Center," December 23, 1927, KFA.

41 Goldman was vice-chair of the committee in charge of English press relations to greet a delegation of distinguished Orthodox rabbis, including Rabbi Abraham Isaac Kook, who visited Cleveland in 1924. Committee stationery preserved in KFA.

42 "Jewish Center Week Dedication Exercises and Festivities, October Twenty-Second to Twenty-Eighth, Nineteen-Hundred Twenty-Two," KFA. On Wolsey, see "Wolsey, Louis," ECH, accessed October 26, 2015, http://ech.case.edu/cgi/article.pl?id=WL3; on Silver, see Ofer Shiff, *The Downfall of Abba Hillel Silver and the Foundation of Israel* (Syracuse: Syracuse University Press, 2014). Cf. also "Rabbi Abba Hillel Silver," accessed October 26, 2015, http://www.clevelandjewishhistory.net/silver/.

43 Wiesenfeld, *Jewish Life in Cleveland*, 67–68; this attempt to found a rival newspaper was predictably heavily disparaged in the *Yiddishe Velt*. See JW, October 13, 1922, KFA.

In March 1923, Katz and his colleagues continued the protest against mixed seating by orchestrating a petition campaign by Jewish Center members against the innovation. Katz's Committee of 100 printed a poster consisting of a collection of photographs of the signed petitions of more than 160 people who claimed to be "members in good standing" of the Jewish Center and who demanded "in accordance with our rights that the services in this congregation be held in accordance with the orthodox laws . . . we protest against the attempt to violate our constitution."[44]

The next stage of the conflict centered on the synagogue's constitution. According to Abraham Katz's narrative:

> In 1923 they called a meeting suddenly. . . . Behind my back Rabbi Goldman sends a notice to adopt a constitution, because they said and thought that no one would find this constitution. They said that there was no such thing as a constitution. . . . On that very night, July 31, 1923 . . . the constitution came into our hands and when the meeting on Aug. 6 came into effect, we filed our protest immediately and told him it is illegal. After they refused to permit us to read our constitution we said, "Rabbi the only reason you want to adopt a new constitution tonight is because you know that our constitution contains a clause that you can never have men and women sit together in our congregation unless unanimously voted against."[45]

Katz was referring to a constitutional document he alleged had been adopted by the congregation on March 18, 1917, shortly after the formal merger of Anshe Emeth and Beth Tefilo. Katz's opponents, including Rabbi Goldman and President Bialosky, categorically denied that the congregation had adopted any constitution in 1917. Bialosky, to the contrary, asserted in a newspaper article that: "In 1917, a committee was appointed to draft a constitution. The document was so preposterous that the committee never had the courage to present it to the congregation and it was never presented to it."[46]

Rabbi Goldman's partisans further asserted that in 1919 the Jewish Center appointed a committee to draft a constitution, but that the committee

---

44 Poster preserved in KFA.
45 Abraham A. Katz, draft of speech to the Union of Orthodox Jewish Congregations of America, 6, KFA.
46 Clipping preserved in KFA.

never reported. According to this narrative, during the three years between 1919 and 1922, the congregation's attention was so distracted by the major fundraising efforts necessary to pay for the new building that the constitutional issue was not raised. Furthermore, according to this narrative, it is only when Rabbi Goldman was elected and discovered that the Jewish Center did not possess a constitution that the effort to adopt one was revived.[47] Katz, not surprisingly, categorized this narrative as a complete falsehood serving the purposes of the pro-mixed-seating faction. Katz and his supporters successfully thwarted the move for the adoption of a new constitution in 1923 and 1924. However, in the congregational election held after the High Holidays of 1924, the pro-mixed-seating faction seized a majority of the board. Under these changed circumstances, the new constitution was finally approved and ratified on November 25, 1924. Whereas the 1917 constitutional document spoke of "Orthodox Judaism," it is no surprise that the constitution proposed by Rabbi Goldman stated, in article two, that: "The object of this congregation is to maintain Conservative Judaism." The way now seemed open to effect the change for the next major holiday, Passover of 1925.

The conflict within the Jewish Center spawned several mediation efforts. Rabbi Herbert Goldstein, testifying in 1927, recalled that in 1923, when he was in Cleveland, "I made it my special business to see [Goldman] twice in the hope that this case might not be brought to the courts." In March 1925, Agudas ha-Rabbonim, a body composed of European-trained Orthodox rabbis in North America, summoned Rabbi Goldman to a rabbinical court hearing (*din Torah*).[48] It was a summons that Goldman ostentatiously ignored.[49] The Agudas ha-Rabbonim further advised Katz to turn to Cyrus Adler, president of the Jewish Theological Seminary, "whom we know to be an honest and honorable man who loves peace."[50] Katz went to New York to see Adler, who convinced him "that the Seminary was founded and at present stands for the preservation of traditional Judaism."[51] Adler wrote to Rabbi Goldman on March 27, 1925:

> My object in writing you now is to urge you not to put this proposed change into effect at the approaching Passover, as

---

47   Samuel J. Bialosky, "The Cleveland Jewish Center," December 23, 1927, KFA.
48   Copy of the summons, dated 13 Adar 5685 [March 9, 1925], is in KFA.
49   Goldman's reply, "Meshiv ke-Halakha," was published in JW, August 21, 1925, 8.
50   Agudas ha-Rabbonim to Committee of 100, 28 Adar 5685 [March 24, 1925], KFA
51   Abraham Katz to Herbert Goldstein, April 27, 1925, KFA.

it is likely to create a disturbance and a Hillul ha-Shem [desecration of God's name], of which the Center has already had enough. If the attitude of the Seminary means anything to you, it would be not at any time to force or even encourage changes in the ritual or the practice of a Congregation.[52]

Sam Rocker, editor of Cleveland's Yiddish-language newspaper, the *Yiddishe Velt,* wrote in an editorial published on May 22, 1925 that he too had attempted to facilitate an out-of-court settlement. The Union of Orthodox Jewish Congregations of America in a 1927 press release also mentioned its attempts to effect reconciliation in 1925 at the Mizrachi convention in Cleveland as well as in November 1927, when the court case was pending.[53]

However, no persuasion could prevent Rabbi Goldman and his partisans from going forward with mixed seating during the Passover holiday of 1925. At least initially, the results were not pretty. The Committee of 100 planned a demonstration in the synagogue on the first day of Passover, April 9, 1925.[54] While apparently that demonstration was not held, according to Katz's account, none of the regular Torah readers could be persuaded to perform in the synagogue that Passover, and Goldman had to do the job himself. Additionally, only a few women could be persuaded to come down from the balcony and sit among the men. On the Sabbath after Passover, however, the conflict grew intense, and there was an Orthodox protest that turned violent. As Katz described the incident:

> Mr. S. Weinzimmer . . . before the opening of the ark, stood in front of the ark . . . his intention . . . being to prevent the reading of the Torah as a protest. . . . Rabbi Goldman . . . forcibly attempted to shove him aside and take out the Torah. Mr. Aurbach . . . jumped up on the platform and grabbed hold of Mr. Weinzimmer; thereupon a dozen men jumped up upon the platform, and I regret to say blows were exchanged. Upon the

---

52 Ira Robinson, ed., *Cyrus Adler: Selected Letters* (Philadelphia: Jewish Publication Society, 1985), vol. 2, 113–114. Katz recalled what Adler said to him: "Such questions are not voted on by majorities. . . . I beg of you, if you have the Jewish Theological Seminary at heart, do not bring men and women together for services at least during the Passover." Draft speech to the Union of Orthodox Jewish Congregations of America, 4, KFA.

53 Cf. R. G[omborow], letter to the editor of the *Jewish Times* [Baltimore], November 30, 1927, KFA.

54 Committee of 100 to Members who Signed Protest Cards, April 7, 1925, KFA.

platform . . . was also Mr. A. Jaffee who told the rabbi he was a "*Messes Umodiach*" [one who incites to sin].[55]

Because of these disturbances, several men were formally told that they were no longer welcome to worship in the Jewish Center.[56]

During the High Holidays of 1925, the Orthodox dissidents were forced to continue their protest outside the Jewish Center by holding separate services in the old Anshe Emeth building.[57] During their absence, Rabbi Goldman took the opportunity to eliminate the priestly blessing from the liturgy. Katz recalls that:

> During the absence of our protesting members during the high holidays, Rabbi Goldman took advantage and eliminated duchan, kneeling even of the cantor, reciting of kaddish by individuals. On Sukkot two kohanim attempted to duchan. The rabbi ordered the congregation to be seated, the cantor to ignore the kohanim and he himself sat through it all with his head turned away.[58]

Going to Court

The conflict culminated in a 1925 civil suit in the Cleveland Court of Common Pleas, initiated by Abraham Katz and twelve co-plaintiffs against Rabbi Goldman and the Jewish Center leadership. It alleged that the congregation's constitution provided that the congregation had to remain Orthodox. The amended plaintiffs' petition, filed in May 1926, accused Rabbi Goldman of instituting mixed seating as well as other ritual changes, including forbidding the priestly blessing during the holidays, forbidding the ceremony of kneeling during Yom Kippur, and eliminating additional poetic hymns (*piyyutim*). The petition further accused Rabbi Goldman of having stated publicly that God did

---

55 Abraham Katz to Leon Spitz, August 3, 1925, KFA.

56 M. D. Shanman, Jewish Center president, to S. Weinzimmer, April 19, 1925; G. L. Silberman, Jewish Center secretary, to E. Gerson, April 23, 1925; S. Bialosky, Jewish Center acting president, to S. Weinzimmer, April 4, 1926, KFA.

57 Yiddish handbill of the administrative committee representing the Committee of 100, KFA.

58 Abraham Katz to Herbert Goldstein, October 19, 1925, marked "draft," KFA.

not give the Torah at Mount Sinai and having belittled and ridiculed the great religious figures of Israel.

Goldman's response to the charges against him and the Jewish Center leadership argued that the Jewish Center was not incorporated to uphold "Orthodox" Judaism but rather "traditional" Judaism, a term used by Orthodox, Conservative, and Reform Jews alike. Furthermore, he contended that there was no governing body of "Jewish churches" able to enforce "Orthodoxy." Moreover, since Judaism never possessed a rigid definition of creed, the term "Orthodox" had no meaning other than in connection with "ritual and practice."

Goldman maintained that the number of Jewish Center members who actually complained about the changes in the congregation was no more than twenty out of a membership of eleven hundred and that some of the plaintiffs were not in fact members in good standing. The Jewish Center's services on Sabbath morning, he contended, continued to be the most highly attended in Cleveland, with most of the attendants being "Orthodox Jews."

Rabbi Goldman tried to define an "Orthodox Jew" fairly narrowly, as someone insisting on the rigid observance of Jewish customs and practices both outside the synagogue as well as within. This definition would exclude almost all Cleveland Jews—for example, Orthodox law prohibits shaving, yet "the rabbis of this congregation are shaven as are the members and even the plaintiffs." Rabbi Goldman thus denied that the plaintiffs, all of whom shaved and some of whom were known to conduct business on the Sabbath, were in fact "actuated by a desire to uphold the doctrines of Orthodox Judaism."

On the specific issue of mixed seating, Rabbi Goldman pointed out that whereas the Orthodox practice was to seat women not merely separately in a gallery but also to have the gallery curtained off, the Jewish Center, prior to any changes, had women seated separately but in an *uncurtained* gallery; therefore, the innovation of mixed seating on the main floor had not taken the congregation away from a state of "Orthodox" practice.[59]

It is also interesting to examine the congregation's official response to the suit, for its self-justification illustrates the extent to which "Orthodox" congregations and individuals in Cleveland had been subject to "Reform" influences:

> It is true that our congregation was founded sixty years ago,
> but for more than a quarter of a century it has been moving
> in the direction of what is generally known as Conservative

---

59 Amended plaintiffs' petition, filed in May 1926, KFA.

Judaism. . . . Some twenty years ago we engaged as our spiritual leader the late Rabbi Samuel Margolies, who was known to shave, to eat without a hat, and seldom if ever attended daily services. Our congregation never pretended to be Orthodox. We have had late Friday evening service for more than a decade. We have had religious school and confirmation of boys and girls together for about fifteen years. . . . Ours was also one of the first congregations to join the United Synagogue of America. In 1921 prior to Rabbi Goldman's coming to our congregation we considered a merger with a well-known Conservative congregation in Cleveland.[60]

The suit against Rabbi Goldman and the Jewish Center, the putative issue of which had become a definition of Orthodoxy, attracted both national and worldwide attention.[61] In January 1928, however, Judge Homer Powell of the Court of Common Pleas dismissed the suit, ruling that the court had no jurisdiction over what amounted to a purely religious matter.[62]

The Orthodox committee appealed the decision and initially seemed to have won when, in July 1929, the Court of Appeals reversed the decision of the Common Pleas Court and granted a temporary injunction for the Orthodox group against the board of trustees of the Jewish Center and Rabbi Goldman, enjoining them from using the synagogue as a Conservative house of worship pending a retrial. The decision was based on the appellate court's acceptance of the plaintiffs' contention that the issue was not a purely religious matter but that the synagogue was a trust, formed for Orthodox purposes, and that its trustees, without violating their trust, could not change the synagogue ritual from Orthodox to Conservative.[63]

---

60 "Cleveland Center Leaders Reply to Orthodox Charges in Well Known Controversy," JTA, November 20, 1927, accessed February 16, 2015, http://www.jta.org/1927/11/20/archive/cleveland-center-leaders-reply-to-orthodox-charges-in-well-known-controversy.

61 "Testimony to Establish 'What is Orthodoxy' Will Be Presented in Courts," JTA, November 4, 1927, accessed February 16, 2015, http://www.jta.org/1927/11/04/archive/testimony-to-establish-what-is-orthodoxy-will-be-presented-in-courts.

62 "Cleveland Jewish Center Case Thrown out of Court by Ruling of Judge Powell," JTA, January 18, 1928, accessed February 16, 2015, http://www.jta.org/1928/01/18/archive/cleveland-jewish-center-case-thrown-out-of-court-by-ruling-of-judge-powell.

63 "Changing Orthodox to Conservative Synagogue Trust Breach Court Rules," JTA, July 22, 1929, accessed February 16, 2015, http://www.jta.org/1929/07/22/archive/changing-orthodox-to-conservative-synagogue-trust-breach-court-rules.

However, the Orthodox victory was short-lived, because within a couple of months the Jewish Center brought the issue before another appellate court, which concurred with the original decision that the case centered on "a strictly ecclesiastical question" and again dismissed the suit.[64] The Orthodox side once again appealed to the Supreme Court of Ohio, which, in December 1929, upheld the previous appellate decision and thus ended several years of litigation.[65] The Jewish Center was to continue to be Conservative and not Orthodox,[66] though Goldman left Cleveland for a congregation in Chicago before the legal issue had definitively closed. Goldman's biographer is puzzled about the reason for his leaving,[67] but it would seem that the Orthodox opposition to him personally had caused him a great deal of bitterness. Goldman seems to have reciprocated and harbored what Leon Wiesenfeld describes as a virulent hatred of the Orthodox, whom, "if he had the power, he would have exiled . . . to Siberia, as long as not to have them in Cleveland."[68]

The Rabbinic Confrontation in New York, November 1927

Much of the attention paid to the Jewish Center case outside of Cleveland hinged on an event that occurred not in Cleveland, but in New York City at the beginning of November 1927. In preparation for the trial, depositions were taken from a series of Orthodox rabbis and leaders in connection with the case. These men directly confronted not merely Goldman's lawyer but Goldman personally, who was, "given all the latitude he wanted in conducting examinations" and apparently conducted the cross examination himself.[69]

---

64 "Court Dismisses Appeal on Cleveland Center Case," JTA, September 30, 1929, accessed February 16, 2015, http://www.jta.org/1929/09/30/archive/court-dismisses-appeal-on-cleveland-center-case.

65 "Appeal to Supreme Court in Jewish Centre Dispute," JTA, November 17, 1929, accessed February 15, 2015, http://www.jta.org/1929/11/17/archive/appeal-to-supreme-court-in-jewish-centre-dispute; "Supreme Court Rules for Reform Wing in Cleveland Center," JTA, December 15, 1929, accessed February 16, 2015, http://www.jta.org/1929/12/15/archive/supreme-court-rules-for-reform-wing-in-cleveland-center.

66 The congregation is still a major Conservative congregation in Cleveland, now known as the Park Synagogue. See the congregation's website, accessed May 1, 2022, https://www.parksynagogue.org/.

67 Weinstein, Solomon Goldman, 17.

68 Wiesenfeld, Jewish Life in Cleveland, 73–74.

69 R. G[omborow], letter to the editor of the Jewish Times [Baltimore], November 30, 1927, clipping in KFA.

Giving depositions in support of the suit against Goldman and the Jewish Center were seven Orthodox rabbis. They included Eliezer Silver (1882–1968),[70] Bernard Revel (1885–1940),[71] Gedaliah Bublick (1875–1948), Herbert Goldstein (1890–1970), Moses Sebulun Margolies (1851–1936), Bernard Drachman (1861–1945),[72] and Leo Jung (1892–1987).[73] As a group they included both the predominantly Yiddish-speaking, European-trained Orthodox rabbinate, organized in the Agudas ha-Rabbonim, and the nascent English-speaking "Modern Orthodox" rabbinate. The first group included Rabbis Silver and Margolies as prominent members, and the latter was composed of Rabbis Goldstein, president of the Union of Orthodox Jewish Congregations of America; Jung, whose Jewish Center in Manhattan was a flagship institution of acculturated Orthodoxy; Drachman, former faculty member of Jewish Theological Seminary; and Revel, head of the Rabbi Isaac Elchanan Theological Seminary, which was the predominant institution for the training of American Orthodox rabbis. Also included was Gedaliah Bublick, editor of *Tageblatt*, the New York Yiddish daily that catered to an Orthodox readership.

Rabbis favorable to the defendant did not come to give depositions, though lawyer R. Gomborow asserted that, "We have asked members of the Jewish Theological Seminary faculty to come and testify, but they declined." Goldman and his lawyer were not alone, however. Gomborow further asserts that at Goldman's side sat his brother-in-law, Mr. Lefkowitz, a Brooklyn attorney; Rabbi Elias Solomon (1879–1956),[74] president of the United Synagogue of America; Rabbi Louis Finkelstein (1895–1991)[75] of the Jewish Theological

---

70   Aaron Rakeffet-Rothkoff, *The Silver Era in American Jewish Orthodoxy: Rabbi Eliezer Silver and His Generation* (New York: Yeshiva University Press, 1981).

71   Aaron Rakeffet-Rothkoff, *Bernard Revel: Builder of American Jewish Orthodoxy* (Philadelphia: Jewish Publication Society, 1972).

72   Jeffrey Gurock, "From Exception to Role Model: Bernard Drachman and the Evolution of Jewish Religious Life in America, 1880–1920," *American Jewish History* 76, no. 4 (June 1987): 456–484.

73   On Rabbi Jung, see Maxine Jacobson, *Modern Orthodoxy in American Judaism: The Era of Rabbi Leo Jung* (Boston: Academic Studies Press, 2016). Originally there were more witnesses considered for the depositions. Beside the men whose testimony has been preserved, we have the names of Rabbi Selzer of the Agudas ha-Rabbonim, Dr. I. L. Bril, Mr. Sobel, Mr. Lipkowitz, Mr. Scheinberg, and Captain Naftali Taylor Phillips of New York's Shearith Israel. The transcripts of the depositions are to be found in KFA.

74   On Rabbi Solomon, see "Elias Louis Solomon," Jewish Virtual Library, accessed October 26, 2015, http://www.jewishvirtuallibrary.org/jsource/judaica/ejud_0002_0018_0_18822.html.

75   Michael B. Greenbaum, *Louis Finkelstein and the Conservative Movement: Conflict and Change* (New York: Jewish Theological Seminary Press, 2009).

Seminary; Rabbi Jacob Kohn (1881–1968); and "several other Conservative rabbis."[76] Though none of the pro-Goldman rabbis spoke for the record, they apparently did intervene. For example, during the cross-examination of Rabbi Jung, Rabbi Goldman tried to refute the charge that he had excluded Orthodox rabbis from his Jewish Center Forum by stating that no rabbis spoke at that forum. However, Rabbi Finkelstein presumably corrected him, for Goldman then stated: "I wish to make a correction. I have just been reminded that at one of the Forums Doctor Louis Finkelstein spoke."

The Plaintiffs' Issues

The rabbinical depositions were meant to bolster the Orthodox case, and the deponents certainly did their best to fulfill expectations. Rabbi Jung testified first. The first substantive question asked him was, "What do you say is Orthodox Judaism?" Over Rabbi Goldman's objection, Rabbi Jung replied that Orthodox Judaism was "based upon faith in the divine origin of the Torah and loyalty to *din Torah* as expressed in Talmud, Codes, and responsa." He defined Reform Judaism, to the contrary, as not recognizing the divine origin of the law or its binding force and "represents a definite break with Jewish tradition and faith."[77] There were no really significant additions by the others to this definition.

When Rabbi Jung was asked concerning Conservative Judaism he stated that it constituted a form of moderate Reform distinguished by an attitude of reasonable fidelity toward Jewish law but with a tendency toward compromise. He saw the salient differences of Conservative Judaism with Orthodoxy to be the sitting of men and women together and, less often, organs and mixed choirs. Rabbi Drachman reiterated the identification of Conservative Judaism as one variety of Reform. He added that Conservatism was "the same as Reform in its principles but it has not carried out the logical conclusions of them to the same degree." According to Drachman, while Conservative Jews have not necessarily rejected divine revelation, they did feel they had the right to modify "those things which are . . . or seem to be of Rabbinical origin," and thus they shortened the ritual in a way contrary to Orthodox law. Rabbi Drachman further added that "Reform also claims the right to interpret

---

76 R. G[omborow], letter to the editor of the *Jewish Times* [Baltimore], November 30, 1927, clipping in KFA.

77 A motion was made by the defendant to exclude this answer.

Judaism according to its own view." Rabbi Goldstein in his deposition went somewhat farther and was of the opinion that Conservative Judaism "in practice does not believe in the revealed religion." For Gedalaiah Bublick, Conservative Judaism was "Reform from beginning to end . . . sometimes it maintains it is Orthodoxy, whereas it is Reformed." Bernard Revel, while he did not think that the Conservative Jews had one mode of worship or set of customs, felt that "they arrogate to themselves the right to make changes and to modify rules and customs in accordance with time and place." Rabbi Silver thought of Conservative Judaism as "the first step of Reform." Rabbi Jung did not see any difference between traditional and Orthodox Judaism. Bublick had a highly interesting take on traditional Judaism, much of which is crossed out in the transcript as follows:

> Traditional Judaism is a new term that is not clear. It was never used until a few years ago. ~~It can mean everything; it can mean nothing.~~ To me Traditional Judaism as to any Orthodox Jew, *is only one kind of traditional* means Judaism—that is Orthodox Judaism, Judaism of tradition, ~~but as I understand, there are some who deviate from Orthodoxy and they choose to call their kind under the name of Traditional Judaism because it gives them a clear field to deviate from Orthodox Judaism, and still maintain that they are some kind of Orthodox.~~

The United Synagogue was an institution that all the deponents agreed was ambiguous in its ideology. For Rabbi Jung, it was composed of some Orthodox synagogues along with a majority of congregations that permitted the moderate reforms he associated with Conservatism. Rabbi Drachman concurred that it "represents the conservative and Orthodox views to a certain extent." Bublick stated that it contained Conservative congregations "unless there are some Orthodox congregations . . . that didn't learn yet the difference between Conservative and Orthodox Judaism." For Rabbi Silver, the United Synagogue was "partly Orthodox by mistake."

One of the major points of the deponents was the non-legitimacy of the Jewish Theological Seminary with respect to Orthodoxy. Thus, Rabbi Jung declared that the seminary was "definitely not known as Orthodox," and he did not believe that its graduates received formal rabbinic ordination (*semikha*). Rabbi Drachman, who had been on the seminary's faculty in its earlier years, differentiated between the Jewish Theological Seminary of Rabbi Sabato Morais (1823–1897), which was "strictly Orthodox," and the later seminary.

Rabbi Goldstein, who was a 1914 graduate of the seminary, stated that it recommended its men to Orthodox, Conservative, and Reform congregations alike, and condemned the seminary's faculty and students for ritual infractions such as not washing and saying the blessings before meals and not reciting the benediction after dining.

Rabbi Mordecai Kaplan (1881–1983), a Jewish Theological Seminary faculty member who had publicly and ostentatiously abandoned Orthodoxy, was characterized by Rabbi Drachman as "a scholar and an able man in many ways" who was nonetheless "fundamentally unorthodox, anti-religious." Bublick thought Kaplan was "now the exponent of conservative Judaism, anti-Orthodox in every respect." Rabbi Margolies added an ironic comment on his experience with Kaplan as his former assistant rabbi: "He was at one time junior rabbi of my congregation—a junior rabbi gives sermons, but to decide questions they have senior rabbis."

Goldman's Cross-Examination

Rabbi Goldman had a strategy for his cross-examination, which was closely related to the strategy he took in his formal response to the charges against him. He did not appear interested in those rabbis he considered closest to Eastern European Orthodoxy and thus conducted no cross-examination of Rabbis Margolies, Revel, or Silver. He concentrated his questions largely on those Orthodox rabbis with "modern" congregations. His goal was to show that they were no more "Orthodox" than he was, because all of them deviated in some way from the strict rules of Orthodox halakhah. Thus, one of the key points he was anxious to make was to contextualize his own actions as rabbi with what he contended was the widespread violation of "Karo's Code" (*Shulḥan Arukh*)[78] by congregations that claimed to be Orthodox. Thus, in his cross-examination of Rabbi Jung, Goldman pointed out that Jung's synagogue, the Jewish Center in New York, had an elevator that operated on the Sabbath. Rabbi Jung admitted that this was so but countered that in the Orthodox rabbinical opinions he had sought, operating the elevator with a gentile operator was not contrary to halakhah.[79]

---

78 On the Shulḥan Arukh, see Elimelech Westreich, "Shulḥan 'arukh," The YIVO Encyclopedia of Jews in Eastern Europe, accessed October 26, 2015, http://www.yivoencyclopedia.org/article.aspx/Shulhan_arukh.

79 This decision was rendered by Rabbi Moses Margolies. Ferziger, *Beyond Sectarianism*, 45.

Rabbi Goldman also attempted to get Rabbi Jung to admit that Orthodox halakhah "prohibits the reading of all literature which we would include in the category of belles lettres." Rabbi Jung in his response sought to limit this ban to "the reading of any literature that harps on 'sex stuff.'"

Rabbi Goldman raised the issue of the *Shulḥan Arukh's* prohibition of prayer in the presence of women with uncovered heads and dressed in décolleté fashions. He asked Rabbi Jung: "Is it not true that in many Orthodox synagogues women come so dressed?" Jung was finally compelled to answer this question by admitting that, "Rabbis have no power to enforce Jewish law." However, he added: "In my own [congregation] they would frown upon any woman who comes to a Jewish ceremony not properly dressed. It has happened more than once that a lady was asked to leave because not properly dressed."

With Rabbi Drachman, Rabbi Goldman explored the widely practiced custom of shaving, which many members of Orthodox synagogues practiced despite its being contrary to halakhah. This forced Drachman to attempt to differentiate between "Orthodox" and "religious" where "Orthodoxy is an expression of a view concerning a certain concept of Jewish authority," and "religious" is the actual practice: "A man who wishes to be Orthodox in principle and religious in practice will not shave. While I uphold the principle of the authority of Jewish law, I am not going to interfere with people in their private affairs."

Rabbi Goldman queried Rabbi Drachman on the prevalence of violators of the Sabbath becoming members of Orthodox congregations, to which Drachman replied: "I am acquainted with a large number of members who personally are not observant yet they would not permit the Orthodox rules and practices [of the synagogue] to be touched."

Rabbi Goldman's cross-examination of Rabbi Drachman also explored the issue of men and women shaking hands, which Drachman admitted to be prohibited by halakhah, but added: "Other principles, however, make that [prohibition] a little less rigid and establish as good conduct the relations between men and women as they are customarily observed in various countries."

Rabbi Goldman zeroed in on the key issue of mixed seating in the synagogue and asked where specifically was a prohibition of mixed seating as opposed to "social intercourse [between men and women] in general" to be found in halakhah. Rabbi Jung responded that while "there has been throughout Jewish history the understanding and practice that men and women do not sit together at worship," he was not prepared to comment on the question of the specific prohibition and finally admitted:" I will have to look it up. Not prepared to answer this."

Rabbi Goldman further queried Rabbi Jung on the prevalence of mixed social dancing at Orthodox synagogue functions, the halakhic prohibition of which historian Jeffrey Gurock indicates was "widely honored in the abuse" in this era.[80] Pressed on this issue, Rabbi Jung admitted: "I would rather not see it—there is no definite law prohibiting dancing. It seems to me not in accord with Jewish practice. It is one of those cases where the rabbi cannot enforce his view."

Rabbi Goldman concluded this line of questioning with this statement, which received an objection but not an answer from Rabbi Jung: that the *Shulḥan Arukh, Oraḥ Ḥayyim* 529:4 prohibits mingling of men and women on any occasion of social amusement.

In his cross-examination of Rabbi Drachman, Rabbi Goldman also focused on the issue of rabbinic authority and got Drachman to admit that there was no person or group of rabbis in the United States that the American Jews recognized as a general authority. As Rabbi Drachman put it: "The conditions in America are such that there is no official status of that kind," though he also added that "there is such a thing as personal recognition and recognition of organizations." Rabbi Drachman further explained:

> We live in countries where rigid conformity is not possible. The Western Rabbi has to exercise good judgement. That does not mean that the law is abrogated but we must consider, in particular cases, whether it is better to carry it out or to deviate from it. People who think that because of this Orthodox Judaism is not in force do not appreciate its true spirit and are seeking an excuse for actually overthrowing it.

What the situation ultimately meant to Rabbi Drachman is that one needs to differentiate between Judaic practice within the synagogue and outside it. Whereas it might be possible and even necessary to compromise in other areas of life, such compromises "certainly may not be extended to the synagogue."

Rabbi Goldman also brought up an issue dividing Orthodox rabbis—that is, whether the separate women's seating in the synagogue, often in a balcony, had to be curtained off as well. Rabbi Drachman admitted that there was indeed a difference in interpretation among Orthodox rabbis on that issue.

---

80 Gurock, *Orthodox Jews in America*, 8.

Goldman also responded to a charge that he had stated from the Jewish Center pulpit "that the story of the flood as given in the Pentateuch is a myth and that no boy of 12 years of age would believe it." Rabbi Goldman thus asked Gedaliah Bublick: "What is your basis for assuming that a Conservative Rabbi denied Torah min Hashomayim" (divine origin of the Torah)? Bublick answered that while "Conservative Judaism has no books or constitution. . . . I know that here and there rabbis say there is no Torah or Jewish law including yourself." It is at that point that Rabbi Goldman asked Bublick the most iconic question of the entire session, "Do you believe that Aton Balaam [Balaam's ass] spoke?" Goldman asked a follow-up question: "Do you think there is no difference from the traditional point of view between the story of the flood and the story of Aton Balaam?" Bublick could only answer: "I say that a Rabbi who denies from the pulpit the story of the flood is reformed or conservative."

A Jewish "Monkey Trial"

The story of the rabbinic depositions was almost immediately leaked to the press, which knew well how to sensationalize the story. The headline of an article in the *Tog* of November 3, 1927 says it all: "Balaam's Ass, the Flood, and the question can a rabbi kiss a bride under the Wedding Canopy discussed in a hearing against Rabbi Solomon Goldman of Cleveland."

Connections were inevitably and widely made between this court case and the "Monkey Trial" of 1925, which was portrayed as a confrontation between science/progress and religion/traditionalism—to the decided detriment of the latter.[81] Thus, an English language Jewish newspaper on December 9, 1927 spoke of:

> another Monkey Trial to take place in Cleveland before a non-Jewish tribunal to determine whether a certain congregation of that city has violated the fundamentals of Orthodoxy . . . the old stand-patters say you are wrong, dear Rabbi, you have no right or authority to kiss the bride . . . men and women should not sit together in a truly Orthodox synagogue.[82]

---

81 Among the many books on this trial, see Edward J. Larson, *Summer for the Gods: The Scopes Trial and America's Continuing Debate Over Science and Religion* (Cambridge: Harvard University Press, 1998).

82 "Another Monkey Trial—This Time It's Jewish," December 9, 1927, KFA.

Abraham Katz could only bemoan the press coverage in general to Rabbi Goldstein: "All so called facts which the other side . . . state in the press are downright falsehoods."[83] Katz asserted that his opponents had "spread the falsehood in various papers that we were going to have a 'monkey trial' when it is they who introduced the religious issue."[84]

A Clearer Drawing of the Battle Lines?

The Jewish Center case and the wide publicity it received ultimately served to more clearly demarcate the then-often-fuzzy line between "Orthodox" and "Conservative" in North American Judaism. This outcome was acutely sensed by Mordecai Kaplan in 1927, and it reinforced his feeling that the time had come to definitely sever ties with Orthodoxy. As he put it:

> Thanks to the aggressiveness of Jewish fundamentalists, those who belong to the large body of adjectiveless Jews are now realizing their mistake. . . . They are being forced to make their position clear. They must take a definite stand with regard to the traditional attitude toward the Torah. They must formulate the principle or the principles they intend to follow in the changes which they want to introduce into their ceremonial practices as Jews. The bootlegging of innovations will have to be stopped. In other words, they will have to accept the logical and moral consequences that follow from being a distinct party in Judaism. . . . Both the orthodox and the Reformists are gradually forcing us to assume the name Conservative.[85]

Kaplan reiterated this conviction in his journal on July 22, 1929. Reacting to the news of the first court of appeal that seemed to uphold the Orthodox side, he stated:

> I am very happy that the decision of the court made it clear that Conservatism cannot hide under the skirt of Orthodoxy.

---

83 Abraham Katz to Herbert Goldstein, January 3, 1928, KFA.
84 Abraham Katz to Herbert Goldstein, August 8, 1929, KFA.
85 Cited from I. L. Bril, "In the News: Society for the Advancement of Judaism Review," *Tageblatt* [English section], December 6, 1927, KFA.

Perhaps this decision will have the effect of ultimately breaking up that unnatural alliance between reactionism and progressivism which has paralyzed the Rabbinical Assembly and placed it in a position where it can do absolutely nothing of any account.[86]

For the Orthodox leadership in Cleveland itself, the Jewish Center affair had taught it a somewhat different but no less cogent lesson: that of the weakness of Orthodoxy in its confrontation with its rivals. In 1945, contemplating the impending move of Cleveland's Orthodox synagogues from East 105th Street to Cleveland Heights, Rabbi Israel Porath advised his readers that existing synagogues must combine to create fewer but larger synagogues in the new area. However, he further admonished: "I do not want to advise that we should contemplate a synagogue that is too large and powerful because the experience of the Jewish Center demonstrated that Orthodoxy is not strong enough to protect its interests in time of crisis."[87]

The "Jewish Monkey Trial" certainly did not in and of itself cause the definitive split between Orthodox and Conservative Judaism. It was, however, one of the more important milestones in that process, and its examination allows us to see with greater clarity the fault lines in American Judaism as they were beginning to become more apparent in the early twentieth century.

---

86 Mel Scult, ed., *Communings of the Spirit: The Journals of Mordecai M. Kaplan, 1913–1934* (Detroit: Wayne State University Press, 2001), 346.
87 Israel Porath, "The Second Destruction of Cleveland Orthodox Synagogues" [Yiddish], JW, March 28, 1945, 2.

CHAPTER 5

The New Haven Yeshiva, 1923–1937: An Experiment in American Jewish Education

I. Introduction

At this point in the twenty-first century, the network of Lithuanian-style yeshivot in North America and Israel offering advanced rabbinical studies to Orthodox men is large and expanding.[1] From a scholarly perspective, there is a consensus that the major impact of such institutions in North America began in earnest in the 1940s. Nonetheless, it is relevant to note some important developments in this area in the earlier twentieth century. Of the early institutions of postsecondary yeshiva education in North America, most scholarly attention has been given to the Rabbi Isaac Elchanan Theological Seminary in New York (founded in 1915) and Chicago's Hebrew Theological College (founded in 1922), both of which enjoyed continuity and success in the postwar era.[2]

There were other postsecondary yeshivot founded in the prewar era, however, which did not enjoy such continuity. An example is the yeshiva of Montreal, Canada, founded in the 1920s, which left few documentary

---

1 On yeshivot in America, see William B. Helmreich, *The World of the Yeshiva: An Intimate Portrait of Orthodox Jewry* (Hoboken, NJ: KTAV, 2000); Oscar Z. Fasman, "Trends In The American Yeshiva Today," *Tradition: A Journal of Orthodox Jewish Thought* 9, no. 3 (Fall 1967): 48–64; Jonathan Boyarin, *Yeshiva Days: Learning on the Lower East Side* (Princeton, NJ: Princeton University Press, 2020).
2 Gilbert Klaperman, *The Story of Yeshiva University: The First Jewish University in America* (New York: Macmillan, 1969).

traces.[3] This article tells the story of a yeshiva that was founded in New Haven, Connecticut in 1923, moved to Cleveland, Ohio in 1929, and went out of existence in 1937. It was known as the New Haven Yeshiva, both in its original home in New Haven, as well as in Cleveland. Likely because it had no institutional continuity in the postwar period, the existence of the New Haven Yeshiva has received relatively little attention. However, in the words of William Helmreich, it merits our attention as "the first Mussar yeshiva in the United States, as well as the first yeshiva patterned almost completely after those in Eastern Europe."[4] Its rise, as well as its demise, has much to tell us concerning the development of Orthodox Judaism in North America in the 1920s and 1930s.[5]

II. Creating a Yeshiva in New Haven, 1923–1929

The New Haven Yeshiva was the brainchild of Rabbi Yehuda Heshel ha-Levi Levenberg (1884–1938).[6] He was born in Pilten (Piltenes pilsēta), Courland (now Latvia), then located within the Russian Empire. He studied Torah with Rabbi Shlomo Zalman Sender Kahana Shapira (1851–1923) one of the leading rabbis of Lithuania. Shapira was a disciple of Rabbi Yosef Dov Soloveitchik (1820–1892) as well as his son Rabbi Chaim Soloveitchik (1853–1918). He was also the teacher of Rabbi Aharon Kotler (1892–1962), founder of the important American yeshiva, Beth Medrash Gavoha in Lakewood, New Jersey in 1943.[7] Rabbi Levenberg went on to study at the Slobodka Yeshiva, where he was greatly influenced by its Mussar orientation.[8] He retained his affinity

---

3   Robinson, *Rabbis and Their Community*, 99. Cf. D. Ashkenazi, "Di Montrealer Yeshiva," *Keneder Adler*, October 14, 1921, 4; "A Bazukh in Yeshiva," *Keneder Adler*, August 31, 1925, 5.

4   William B. Helmreich, "Old Wine in New Bottles: Advanced Yeshivot in the United States," *American Jewish History* 69, no. 2 (December 1979): 24–26. Cf. Ari Z. Zivitofsky, "Torah Shines Forth from New Haven . . . and Cleveland," *Jewish Observer* 36, no. 10 (December 2003): 16–22.

5   On Orthodox Judaism in North America in this era, see Gurock, *Orthodox Jews in America*.

6   On Rabbi Levenberg, see the biography by his son-in-law, Isaac Hirsch Ever: Ever, *Rabbi J. H. Levenberg*; Moshe Sherman, *Orthodox Judaism in America: A Biographical Dictionary and Sourcebook* (Westport, CT: Greenwood Press, 1996), 131–133; Benzion Eisenstadt, *Doros ha-Aḥaronim* (New York, 1914), 213–216.

7   On Rabbi Kahana Shapira, see his page at Geni.com, accessed December 1, 2021, https://www.geni.com/people/Rav-Shlomo-Zalman-Kahana-Shapira/6000000003223832205.

8   On the Slobodka Yeshiva, see Benjamin Brown, "Human Greatness and Human Diminution: Changes in the Mussar Methods in the Slobodka Yeshiva" [Hebrew], in *Yeshivot and Battei Midrash*, ed. Immanuel Etkes (Jerusalem: Shazar, 2007), 244–272; Immanuel Etkes, *Rabbi*

for Slobodka-style Mussar for his entire life. Indeed, after his immigration to the United States Rabbi Levenberg became a leader among Slobodka alumni in North America and served as honorary president of the Histadrut Talmidei Slobodka in the United States.[9]

Rabbi Levenberg came to the United States in 1910, having been sent by the head of the Slobodka Yeshiva, Rabbi Moshe Mordecai Epstein (1866–1933), to collect funds for the yeshiva. He stayed in America, first serving as rabbi in Jersey City, New Jersey. He left Jersey City to become rabbi in New Haven, Connecticut in 1916.[10] In 1920, he was appointed Chief Rabbi (*rav ha-kollel*) of New Haven. Rabbi Levenberg, in association with Rabbi M. D. Sheinkop, conceived the idea of founding a yeshiva in his city that would be unlike any yeshiva founded in North America to that point. The two major yeshivas previously created, the Rabbi Isaac Elchanan Theological Seminary in New York and the Hebrew Theological College of Chicago, were in the major tradition of "Lithuanian" yeshivot founded in Eastern Europe in the nineteenth century. However, neither followed the Mussar tradition emphasized in Rabbi Levenberg's Slobodka Yeshiva. Perhaps spurred by the founding of the Hebrew Theological College in 1922, the first such institution established in North America beyond New York City, Rabbi Levenberg proposed the establishment of a yeshiva in New Haven in 1923 at the annual convention of the Agudas ha-Rabbonim, the association of European-trained Orthodox rabbis in North America, held that year in Lakewood, New Jersey.[11] The yeshiva formally opened on August 12, 1923.[12]

Since Rabbi Levenberg's manifold duties as communal rabbi of New Haven practically precluded him from running a yeshiva entirely on his own,

Israel Salanter and the Mussar Movement—Seeking the Torah of Truth (Philadelphia: Jewish Publication Society, 1993); Shaul Stampfer, *Lithuanian Yeshivas of the Nineteenth Century: Creating a Tradition of Learning* (Oxford: The Littman Library of Jewish Civilization, 2012).

9   Abraham Bick, "A Koventsion fun Bageystere Yunge Frume Iden in Nyu York," *Forverts*, February 18, 1939, 3, 9.

10   *Ha-Yivri* (New York), March 31, 1916, accessed December 2, 2021, https://www.nli. org.il/en/newspapers/haibri/1916/03/31/01/?srpos=1&e=------191-en-20--1--img-txIN%7ctxTI-%d7%9c%d7%a2%d7%95%d7%95%d7%a2%d7%a0%d7%91%d7%a2%d7%a8%d7%92------------1. On the Jewish community in New Haven, see Jonathan Sarna, *Jews in New Haven* (New Haven, CT: Jewish Historical Society of New Haven, 1978).

11   On Agudas ha-Rabbonim, see Jeffrey Gurock, "Resisters and Accommodators: Varieties of Orthodox Rabbis in America, 1886–1983," *American Jewish Archives* (November 1983): 100–187, reprinted in *The American Rabbinate: A Century of Continuity and Change, 1883–1983*, ed. Jacob Rader Marcus and Abraham J. Peck (New York: KTAV, 1985), 10–97; Sherman, *Orthodox Judaism*, 225–236.

12   Zivitofsky, "Torah Shines Forth," 17.

he hired at first Rabbi Yaakov Dov Safsal (1888–1968) and then Rabbi Moshe Scheinkopf as *roshei yeshiva*.[13] They apparently did not stay long, and Rabbi Levenberg then hired Rabbi Shabetai Sheftel Kramer (1875–1942), brother-in-law of Rabbi Levenberg's teacher, Rabbi Moshe Mordecai Epstein, who had arrived in America on November 7, 1924, as *rosh yeshiva*.[14] Rabbi Kramer would be formally "installed in his position" at the New Haven Yeshiva's first ordination ceremony, held on May 10, 1925.[15] In hiring a Slobodka-trained rabbi, Rabbi Levenberg attempted to ensure that the students of his yeshiva would be guided in the spirit of Slobodka.

Rabbi Levenberg's yeshiva became known in Hebrew for its entire existence as *Yeshivas Nyu Haven*[16] in English; it was also referred to as the New Haven Yeshiva, though in its various letterheads it was called in English in the following ways: New Haven College of Talmud, Orthodox Rabbinical Seminary, Rabbinical Seminary and College of Talmud,[17] and Cleveland Rabbinical Seminary.[18]

Within a relatively short time, some thirty-five or forty students had gathered at the New Haven Yeshiva, attracted in large part by the personality and eloquence of Rabbi Levenberg.[19] One former student of the yeshiva, Rabbi Abraham Bick (1913–1990),[20] wrote in 1939 a glowing account of the

---

13 *Ibid*, 18.

14 It is likely that Rabbis Levenberg and Epstein met in 1924 when Rabbi Epstein toured North America in the company of Rabbi Abraham Isaac ha-Kohen Kook (1865–1935). Perhaps the impetus for hiring Rabbi Kramer took place at this time. See Joshua Hoffman, "Rav Kook's Mission to America," accessed December 2, 2021, http://www.ravkooktorah. org/RAV-KOOK-IN-AMERICA.htm. On Rabbi Kramer's date of immigration, I am grateful to Rabbi Yaakov Neuberger of Baltimore, whose email of November 24, 2022 contains a scan of an undated clipping concerning Rabbi Kramer's arrival.

15 "New Haven Graduates First Rabbi Class," *Meriden Record*, May 11, 1925. I am grateful to Rabbi Yaakov Neuberger for this clipping.

16 The yeshiva's Cleveland-period letterhead added the word *de-Klivland*.

17 Yeshiva letterhead preserved in KFA.

18 Isaac H. Ever, ed., *Der Talmudisṭ: Yubileum Zshurnal tsum 50-yerigen Yubileum fun Yehuda Hershl Levenberg* (Cleveland: Ha-Torani—Studenṭen Literaṭen Klub, 1934), English title page.

19 Thirty-five is the number of yeshiva students who signed the protest letter of 1926 (see footnote 22, below); forty is the number of students reported as transferring from New Haven to Cleveland in December 1929. JW, December 13 and 15, 1929.

20 On Rabbi Bick, see Hayyim Rothman, "Rediscovering Radical Rabbi Abraham Bick at the Site of the Former Institut far Yidisher Bildung," *In Geveb: a Journal of Yiddish Studies*, January 12, 2020, accessed December 2, 2021, https://ingeveb.org/blog/rediscovering-radical-rabbi-abraham-bick-at-the-site-of-the-former-institut-far-yidisher-bildung.

atmosphere in the New Haven Yeshiva on Shabbat afternoons, when Rabbi Levenberg presented his Mussar discourse to the yeshiva students:

> The writer of these lines studied a considerable time in the New Haven Yeshiva, and the atmosphere of late Shabbat afternoons toward twilight is still fresh in my memory, when Rabbi Levenberg, deep in thought, would enter the four walls of the cottage on Park Street where the students, would be waiting silently at their study lecterns for his discourse. Rabbi Levenberg would break out in a *niggun*, and in the last play of light and shadow, he would commence his Mussar discourse.[21]

Rabbi Shraga Feivel Mendlowitz of the newly founded Torah Vadaat Yeshiva took some of his boys to the New Haven Yeshiva to experience "a real Beis Midrash on the European model."[22]

While the spiritual and academic side of the New Haven Yeshiva flourished, fundraising for the yeshiva was certainly challenging, given that yeshivot were a novelty in North America and many American Jews had serious doubts about their necessity and viability.[23] The number of Jews in New Haven in the 1920s, estimated at 20,000, did not provide a sufficient donor base for the support of the yeshiva. Likely for fundraising purposes, therefore, the New Haven Yeshiva maintained a representative in New York: Rabbi Mairim Magnes (d. 1948), who was designated in the yeshiva's letterhead as "Executive Chairman."[24] We can also document that the New Haven Yeshiva engaged in fundraising in communities outside New York, such as Cleveland[25] and Portland, Maine.[26] Nonetheless, there are indications that the funds raised for the yeshiva were inadequate to maintain the institution properly.

---

21 Bick, "A Kovension," 9.
22 Yonasan Rosenblum, *Reb Shraga Feivel: The Life and Times of Rabbi Shraga Feivel Mendlowitz, the Architect of Torah in America* (Brooklyn: Artscroll, 2001), 80.
23 Cf. Jeffrey Gurock, "Another Look at the Proposed Merger: Lay Perspectives on Yeshiva-Jewish Theological Seminary Relations in the 1920s," in *Ḥazon Naḥum: Studies in Jewish Law, Thought and History Presented to Dr. Norman Lamm on the Occasion of His Seventieth Birthday*, ed. Norman Lamm, Yaakov Elman, Jeffrey S. Gurock (Hoboken, NJ: KTAV, 1997), 730.
24 Letterhead preserved in KFA.
25 Ever, *Rabbi J. H. Levenberg*, 104–105; Zivitofsky, "Torah Shines Forth," 18.
26 "Orthodox Rabbinical Seminary Dean on Mission to Portland," *Portland Press Herald*, October 28, 1927. I am grateful to Rabbi Yaakov Neuberger for this clipping.

One telling sign of the yeshiva's scarce funding is a letter signed by all thirty-five New Haven Yeshiva students in 1926 protesting inadequate meals:

> Dear Parents' Association!
> Knowing that you have undertaken to work for the welfare of your sons and all the students of the holy yeshivah who are studying here, we hereby deem it necessary to inform you about the current conditions: The cook has little understanding of what cleanliness is and the food is lousy. Although they try to convince us that the quality is sufficient, we know [otherwise] because we and no one else are the ones who are eating the food and experiencing discomfort, and we feel that the situation should be improved immediately. The meat we are served is almost a "poison of death" for our stomachs and many boys need to take medication. A meeting of all the yeshivah boys was convened and we all protested against the kitchen staff and all those who aren't understanding of our situation.[27]

Rabbi Levenberg was acutely aware of his yeshiva's inadequate financial situation, and determined that he would be prepared to move his yeshiva to a larger community if, and when, the right opportunity arose. He expressed these thoughts retrospectively in a letter to his older brother, Rabbi Baruch Zelig Levenberg (1879–1941) of Talsi (Talsu pilsēta), Latvia, dated 9 Shvat, 5690 [February 7, 1930], shortly after the yeshiva's transfer to Cleveland:

> For some time I thought that New Haven was too small to have such an institution, for there is much room to expand and enlarge the yeshiva, and I thought a great deal about this. . . . In the end I reached the conclusion that the good of the yeshiva demanded that we transfer it to a larger community.[28]

Thus, when circumstances brought about what appeared to be a viable offer to relocate the yeshiva in Cleveland in 1929, Rabbi Levenberg was prepared to entertain the idea seriously.

---

27 Dovi Safier and Yehuda Geberer, "The Great Yeshivah Food Protest," *Mishpacha* 830 (September 29, 2020), accessed December 2, 2021, https://mishpacha.com/the-great-yeshivah-food-protest.

28 Ever, *Rabbi J. H. Levenberg*, 178.

III. Transferring the New Haven Yeshiva to Cleveland (August–December 1929)

The documents at our disposal enable us to trace in some detail the process of the negotiations in fall 1929 to transfer the New Haven Yeshiva to Cleveland that resulted in the yeshiva staff and students arriving in Cleveland on December 11, 1929.

The first documented relationship between the Cleveland Jewish community[29] and the New Haven Yeshiva stems from 1926, when a representative of the yeshiva travelled to Cleveland in order to collect funds. This visit spurred the issuing of a call by a group of local Orthodox rabbis, including Chayyim Fishel Epstein (1874–1942), Israel Porath (1886-1974), Ozer Paley, Rabbi Dr. Shraga ha-Kohen Rosenberg (d. 1958), Menaḥem Mendel Eckstein (d. 1946), and Zechariah Sachs, urging the local community to support the New Haven Yeshiva. This resolution was published in Cleveland's Yiddish newspaper, the *Yiddishe Velt*, on July 20, 1926.[30]

However, the push that actually resulted in the yeshiva moving to Cleveland commenced in the summer of 1929. In August, Rabbi Levenberg came to Cleveland as part of a rabbinical delegation that also included Rabbis Joseph Rosen of Passaic, New Jersey (d. 1953), and Menaḥem Judah Guzik of Brooklyn, New York (d. 1943). The rabbis came at the invitation of Cleveland laymen and rabbis, and at the behest of the Agudas ha-Rabbonim, to attempt to resolve a series of disputes on kashrut and other issues that could not be resolved within the community.[31]

As a matter of course, the visiting rabbis would have been invited to address audiences in synagogues and to meet with community leaders. Rabbi Levenberg seems to have impressed many of the leaders of Cleveland's Orthodox community with his eloquence and ideas. It occurred to many Cleveland Jews that Rabbi Levenberg might be an ideal rabbinical leader able to unite the strife-ridden Cleveland Orthodox community and create order in kashrut and other aspects of communal life.[32] Samuel Joshua Rocker (1865–1936),[33] influential publisher of the *Yiddishe Velt*, gave expression to

---

29 On the history of Orthodoxy in Cleveland in this era, see Robinson, "'A Link in the Great American Chain,'" 14–34.

30 Ever, *Rabbi J. H. Levenberg*, 104–105.

31 These issues were present in most immigrant Orthodox communities in North America. For how these issues played out in Montreal, see Robinson, *Rabbis and Their Community*.

32 Ever, *Rabbi J. H. Levenberg*, 159.

33 On Samuel Rocker, see Robinson, "Hasid and Maskil."

this positive community sentiment by publishing an article praising Rabbi Levenberg's eloquence and his ability to move his audiences.[34]

More concretely, the prominent Chibas Jerusalem congregation, founded in 1904 by Lithuanian Jewish immigrants, which had erected in 1926 a magnificent synagogue located in the Glenville neighborhood, then the heart of Cleveland Jewry,[35] made a twofold proposal to Rabbi Levenberg. The proposal involved both Rabbi Levenberg and his New Haven Yeshiva. Rabbi Levenberg himself would become rabbi of Chibas Jerusalem at a generous salary of $5000 a year. In addition, the congregation undertook to support the New Haven Yeshiva by housing it in its synagogue building.

Rabbi Levenberg was inclined to be receptive to this proposal. It corresponded exactly to his ambition to situate his yeshiva in a city like Cleveland whose estimated Jewish population was about four times greater than that of New Haven.[36] He therefore returned to Cleveland during the High Holiday period (October 1929) in order to see if the community's fundraising pledges would make the project viable. Cleveland's response was a "yeshiva fund" of $18,000.[37]

The effort to bring Rabbi Levenberg and the New Haven Yeshiva to Cleveland was directed by a "Ways and Means Committee to Promote the Bringing of the New Haven Yeshiva with Rabbi Levenberg to Cleveland." The Committee's letterhead listed as its address 887 Parkwood Drive, the location of the Chibas Jerusalem synagogue, and it was headed by a Temporary Committee, chaired by M. Rivitz, A. A. Grossman, M. Blitstein, Paul Weinberger, and B. Estreicher.[38] The Temporary Committee's effort was seconded by an editorial in the *Yiddishe Velt*, which stated that "it isn't the city that makes the yeshiva great, but rather the yeshiva that makes the city great."[39] The project was also supported by another *Yiddishe Velt* article published on November 15, 1929, entitled "Ha-Rav Levenberg, der Redner" (Rabbi Levenberg, the Speaker), praising him for his oratorical skills.

---

34 Ever, *Rabbi J. H. Levenberg*, 128.
35 On the Chibas Jerusalem Synagogue, see Jeffrey S. Morris, "Haymarket to the Heights: The Movement of Cleveland's Orthodox Synagogues from Their Initial Meeting Places to the Heights," *Cleveland Memory* 23 (2014), accessed July 14, 2021, https://engagedscholarship. csuohio.edu/clevmembks/23. On the transition of that Jewish neighborhood, see chapter 6 of this volume.
36 In the AJYB 30 (1928–1929): 107–108, the Jewish populations of New Haven and Cleveland were estimated at 22,500 and 85,000, respectively.
37 Ever, *Rabbi J. H. Levenberg*, 160.
38 Letterhead preserved in KFA.
39 Ever, *Rabbi J. H. Levenberg*, 162–165.

That article was written by Pinchas Weinberger, likely identical with Paul Weinberger, a member of the Temporary Committee.

There was, of course, much going on beside laudatory headlines in the Yiddish press. On November 21, Rabbi Levenberg wrote to Abraham A. Katz, a Cleveland Orthodox activist prominent among supporters of the New Haven Yeshiva move,[40] concerning a major complication that would drastically affect the transition of the yeshiva to Cleveland: the serious and prolonged illness of Rabbi Levenberg's wife. Rabbi Levenberg wrote: ". . . upon reaching home, I found the Rebitzin seriously ill and her condition at present shows little improvement. . . . I find this condition uppermost in my mind at present. . . ."[41]

The major outstanding issue before the yeshiva could relocate was nailing down the financial pledges that would enable Rabbi Levenberg, in the face of considerable opposition from the New Haven Jewish community, to move his yeshiva. In a telegram Rabbi Levenberg sent to Abraham Katz on November 27, 1929, he expressed his concern that the promised funds were not yet guaranteed:

> Following telephone conversation wish to say that it is impossible to take any definite steps in regard to moving unless all financial problems will be settled very soon prolonging the matter will I fear involve serious difficulty If a committee is desirous of coming to Newhaven [sic] kindly arrange it as soon as possible so that we can make some definite plans for moving. Stop. This cannot be done unless proper means are furnished.[42]

Presumably in response to Rabbi Levenberg's concerns, a delegation of three Clevelanders did arrive in New Haven. The delegation included Abraham Katz, B. Blum, and N. Gudin.[43] They constituted the Special Committee for Final Arrangements; there was no overlap with the leaders listed in the stationery of the Ways and Means Committee mentioned above. Part of the Cleveland delegation's task in New Haven was to counteract intensive lobbying efforts on the part of New Haven Jews to keep the yeshiva in their city by means of improved financial offers. Another part of the delegation's task was to report to Cleveland Jewry concerning the benefits a yeshiva would give the Cleveland

---

40 On Katz, see more in chapter four of this volume.
41 Judah Levenberg to Abraham Katz, November 21, 1929, KFA.
42 .Telegram, Judah Levenberg to Abraham Katz, November 27, 1929, KFA.
43 Ever, *Rabbi J. H. Levenberg*, 172.

community. B. Blum was thus quoted in an English-language newspaper, the *Jewish Independent*, as stating that, "We have found American boys studying here from all parts of the country, studying and gaining a deeper insight into Jewish knowledge." That same article cited at length Abraham Katz's enthusiastic response to his meeting with the New Haven Yeshiva community:

> Words cannot express our surprise when we saw this great institution and all connected with it. I thought that in America we are building a generation where Jews are Jews in name only, but not in knowledge. Now, since seeing the Rabbinical Seminary in New Haven, which will soon be in Cleveland, I am happy to say that my thought this time was wrong. After speaking with the students and the teachers in this college, I know now that American Jews are bringing up a generation more learned in Jewish knowledge and customs than ever before. I think that if New Haven, with its Jewish population of 15,000 could help in the upkeep of this institution, we, with a population of 100,000 Jews and over in Cleveland and outlying towns should make this Seminary the greatest institution of its kind in the world.

The same article also quoted Katz's statement at a meeting that took place on December 3, 1929:

> The experience of witnessing the enjoyment of the Sabbath in the yeshiva by the students and to see the environment in which they live was certainly the greatest in my life, and the four days I spent there will always remain in my mind because I know now what I did not think possible, and that is that an institution of this kind is in existence.[44]

Two days after the December 3 meeting referred to in the *Jewish Independent* article, on December 5, 1929, Rabbi Levenberg demonstrated that he was still worried that Cleveland's arrangements for funding the yeshiva were still not to his satisfaction. He stated in a letter co-signed by Cleveland representative

---

44 "Yeshiva to be Moved to Cleveland from New Haven within 10 Days," *Jewish Independent*, undated clipping, KFA. From the context, it was published after December 3, 1929.

B. Blum, then present in New Haven: "We would very much appreciate; in fact it is quite essential that more funds be furnished soon in order that we may proceed with this undertaking quickly."[45]

Sometime between December 5 and December 7, the assurances Rabbi Levenberg desired must have been provided. They presumably included a list of some 1500 yeshiva supporters signed up by the organizing committee.[46] Thus, the fateful decision was made to relocate the yeshiva in Cleveland in very short order. On December 7, 1929, Blum in New Haven wrote a three-page letter to Katz in Cleveland, letting him know that next Wednesday, December 11, the "holy yeshiva" will arrive in Cleveland, including the yeshiva's students, its Torah scrolls, and its *roshei yeshiva*, Rabbis Levenberg and Kramer. Blum urged Katz to organize a proper reception for the yeshiva, and to advertise the yeshiva's arrival in all Cleveland English newspapers as well as in a "prominent [*shtarkn*]" advertisement in the *Yiddishe Velt*.[47]

Plans for the yeshiva's December 11 arrival were detailed in a telegram dated December 10, 1929. Rabbi Levenberg and the yeshiva were scheduled to arrive in Cleveland on Wednesday, December 11, 1929 at 9:15 p.m. at the East 105th Street Station of the New York Central Railroad, to be followed by a welcoming ceremony at the Chibas Jerusalem synagogue.[48]

The New Haven Yeshiva arrived in Cleveland on December 11, incurring significant moving expenses, estimated at $2,000.00.[49] However, the train carrying the entourage, which was supposed to arrive at 9:15 p.m., actually arrived two hours late, according to the *Yiddishe Velt* article chronicling the event. Despite this, hundreds of people remained at the 105th Street Station past 11:00 p.m. in order to greet the yeshiva. Over 1,000 attended the celebration held in the Chibas Jerusalem synagogue, and heard speeches by Rabbis Aaron Mordecai Ashinsky (1866–1954) of Detroit, Rabbi Menaḥem Mendel Eckstein (d. 1946) of Cleveland, and Rabbi Levenberg.[50] Rabbi Levenberg spoke several times at the Chibas Jerusalem synagogue on the Shabbat after he arrived in Cleveland, as well as at a mass meeting on Sunday; Cleveland audiences also heard talks by Rabbi Kramer and some of the yeshiva students.[51]

---

45 Judah Levenberg and B. Blum to Abraham Katz, December 5, 1929, KFA.
46 Ever, *Rabbi J. H. Levenberg*, 262.
47 B. Blum (in New Haven) to Abraham Katz (in Cleveland), December 7, 1929, KFA.
48 Telegram preserved in KFA.
49 Ever, *Rabbi J. H. Levenberg*, 257.
50 JW, undated clipping, KFA; *Jewish Independent* 49, no. 17, undated clipping, KFA.
51 JW, December 13 and 15, 1929.

Reflecting on these recent events, Rabbi Levenberg, who had in the meantime returned to New Haven, presumably because of his wife's ill health, stated in a letter dated December 28, 1929:

> We certainly are happy to receive the good and encouraging reports that come pouring in from Cleveland. It's about the only bright star on our dark and dim horizon now. . . . Concerning Mama's condition, the hospital authorities seem to think that her nervous condition is somewhat improved—though from all appearances her physical condition is none too well.[52]

Rabbi Levenberg agreed to the transfer of the yeshiva he had founded in good faith, and came to Cleveland in December 1929 with every intention of settling there. He thus initially brought his family to Cleveland, with the exception of his wife, who remained hospitalized in New Haven. However, on February 7, 1930, he reported to his brother, Baruch Zelig Levenberg, that, "in the approximately two months we have been here, we have still not arranged things. Only this week I brought my family here and I have still not found a proper apartment." Having initiated the career of the New Haven Yeshiva in Cleveland, Rabbi Levenberg felt compelled to return to New Haven by Passover 1930, because of his wife's serious and prolonged illness.[53] Neither he nor anyone else foresaw it at that time, but it would be over two years, until August 1932, that he would find himself able return to Cleveland on a permanent basis. As Rabbi Levenberg stated in the letter to his brother: "Taking the step [to move the yeshiva] was difficult, for there [in New Haven] we were organized, both me and the yeshiva, and now we are exiled in a strange place." Rabbi Levenberg was thus forced to leave the yeshiva "exiled in a strange place" and it began work in its new location under the day-to-day direction of Rabbi Kramer.

IV. The New Haven Yeshiva in Cleveland, 1929–1937

To share his challenges as de facto head of the New Haven Yeshiva in Cleveland, Rabbi Kramer had two junior colleagues. Apparently, the first to join him was

---

52   Judah Levenberg to Morris (addressee's first name), KFA.
53   Ever, *Rabbi J. H. Levenberg*, 172, 182.

Rabbi Samuel Belkin (1911–1976).[54] Rabbi Belkin, then still in his teens, had studied at the Slonim, Mir, and Radun Yeshivas, and received his rabbinical ordination in 1928 at Radun from Rabbi Simon Shkop (1860–1939). When he arrived in America in 1929, Rabbi Belkin renewed his acquaintance with Rabbi Shkop, who was then teaching at the Rabbi Isaac Elchanan Theological Seminary in New York.[55] Rabbi Shkop's return to Poland in fall 1929 created an opening, and Rabbi Belkin was appointed an "interim lecturer" in Talmud to the senior class at Yeshiva College by its President, Rabbi Dr. Bernard Revel (1885–1940). However, Rabbi Belkin was soon recruited by Rabbi Levenberg to be *rosh yeshiva* in the New Haven Yeshiva.[56] By all accounts, Rabbi Belkin was a good, engaging teacher.[57]

Rabbi Belkin was soon joined by another junior *rosh yeshiva*, Rabbi Kramer's son-in-law, Rabbi Jacob Isaac Ruderman (1900–1987), who arrived in Cleveland on 12 Adar 5690 [March 12, 1930].[58] Rabbi Ruderman had studied at the Slobodka Yeshiva and received his rabbinical ordination from Rabbi Moshe Mordecai Epstein of Slobodka in 1926. Rabbi Levenberg's son-in-law and biographer, Rabbi Isaac Hirsch Ever (b. 1913), reports that Rabbis Kramer and Ruderman had a difficult relationship with Rabbi Belkin, causing Belkin to leave the yeshiva after a few months in spring 1930.[59] According to Ever, it was also because of this tense atmosphere that eight New Haven Yeshiva students, a significant portion of the student body, left Cleveland for the Mir Yeshiva in

---

54 Victor B. Geller, *Orthodoxy Awakens: The Belkin Era and Yeshiva University* (Jerusalem, Urim Publications, 2003), 53ff. Cf. "Samuel Belkin," Jewish Virtual Library, https://www.jewishvirtuallibrary.org/samuel-belkin. Jeffrey Gurock notes with some surprise Rabbi Belkin's affiliation with the New Haven Yeshiva: "Belkin's participation in this school warrants further explication. It was certainly an institution quite unlike the university he would later lead." See his *American Jewish Orthodoxy in Historical Perspective* (Hoboken, NJ: KTAV, 1996), 380, n. 131.

55 Geller, *Orthodoxy Awakens*, 56.

56 It seems reasonable to assume that Rabbi Belkin was in contact with Rabbi Levenberg prior to the move to Cleveland. On the other hand, there is no mention of him in press accounts of the move. Rabbi Levenberg did connect Rabbi Belkin with Professor Charles C. Torrey (1863–1956) of Yale, who was instrumental in getting Rabbi Belkin admitted to graduate studies at Brown University. See William Braude, "Samuel Belkin (1911–1976)," *Proceedings of the American Academy for Jewish Research* 44 (1977): xvii–xx.

57 Geller, *Orthodoxy Awakens*, 61; Braude, "Samuel Belkin."

58 Ever, *Rabbi J. H. Levenberg*, 179. On Rabbi Ruderman, see David Katz, "Le-Demuto shel ha-G[aon] R Yaakov Yitshak ha-Levi Ruderman, zt"l," in *Yeshurun: Me'asef Torani* (New York: Makhon Yeshurun, 2006), 134–202.

59 Ever, *Rabbi J. H. Levenberg*, 182.

Poland.[60] While Ever does not specify the cause of these interpersonal difficulties, it is possible to speculate that they stemmed from the fact that Rabbi Belkin was "driven to become westernized," and presumably did not keep secret his ambition to gain an academic degree at an American university, an ambition that Rabbis Kramer and Ruderman would likely have opposed.[61]

During Rabbi Levenberg's lengthy forced absence, the New Haven Yeshiva of Cleveland encountered several serious problems that unraveled much of the original plan for the yeshiva's transfer. First, there was apparently dissatisfaction among the membership of the Chibas Jerusalem Congregation concerning the yeshiva's constant presence in their building, while the rabbi they had hoped to acquire along with the yeshiva remained in New Haven. Clearly, the yeshiva needed to find itself new quarters. Secondly, the financial difficulties brought on by the Great Depression were causing grave financial problems for all Jewish institutions.[62] These same difficulties were certainly present at comparable institutions, like New York's Rabbi Isaac Elchanan Theological Seminary/ Yeshiva College, whose students would have gone hungry but for the kindness and activism of that institution's Women's Auxiliary.[63] Evidently, because of a shortage of funds, some New Haven Yeshiva students were unable to pay their rent and the sheriff evicted them from their quarters.[64] The yeshiva's students were also forced at this time to pay for some of their meals.[65]

These negative developments soon reached the ears of journalist Gedaliah Bublick (1875–1948), who published an article on the New Haven Yeshiva of Cleveland entitled "A-Yeshiva a-Yesoma" (An Orphan Yeshiva) in the New York daily *Morgen Journal* on June 22, 1930. In this article, Bublick accused Rabbi Levenberg, whom he described as "temperamental," of having departed Cleveland suddenly and abandoning the yeshiva "alone in a strange city, among

---

60   Ever, *Rabbi J. H. Levenberg*, 183. One source claims that as many as forty-eight American students attended the Mir Yeshiva. Jack Kugelmass and Jonathan Boyarin, eds., *From a Ruined Garden: The Memorial Books of Polish Jewry* (Bloomington: Indiana University Press, 1998), 138–139, http://shtetlroutes.eu/en/from-american-universities-to-the-polish-yeshivas/. Rabbi Levenberg's son, Shmuel, attended the Grodno Yeshiva in Poland. JW, December 24, 1937; WPA (1937): 137.

61   On Rabbi Belkin's positive attitude toward secular learning, see Geller, *Orthodoxy Awakens*, 58. On the generally negative attitude of yeshivas toward secular learning, see M. Herbert Danzger, *Returning to Tradition: The Contemporary Revival of Orthodox Judaism* (New Haven, CT: Yale University Press, 1989), 150.

62   Ever, *Rabbi J. H. Levenberg*, 249.

63   Geller, *Orthodoxy Awakens*, 174.

64   Ever, *Rabbi J. H. Levenberg*, 183. The congregation converted part of Carmel Hall into a dormitory for thirty-five students. Morris, "Haymarket to the Heights."

65   Ever, *Rabbi J. H. Levenberg*, 262.

strangers . . . an orphan." He reported the impression that Cleveland Jews were wondering how the yeshiva would continue to exist, and that many of them believed that the whole New Haven Yeshiva affair had been a huge mistake.[66]

However, while the New Haven Yeshiva and Rabbi Levenberg had severe detractors within Cleveland's Jewish community,[67] they also retained the loyalty of a group of local supporters, men and women, who did their best to get the yeshiva back on an even keel. The most important thing the yeshiva needed, given that it was no longer completely welcome at the Chibas Jerusalem synagogue, was its own home. Thus, in September 1930, the yeshiva acquired a house at 880 Lakeview Road, a short distance from Chibas Jerusalem, that it would occupy for the rest of its existence. The yeshiva's move into its own home was lauded in an editorial in the *Yiddishe Velt*, published on September 19, 1930. The editorial celebrated the efforts of the local men and women who had stepped forward to rescue the yeshiva in its hour of need.[68]

In these circumstances, Rabbis Kramer and Ruderman had to spend considerable time and effort in fundraising.[69] Much of the fundraising was local, and often involved public programs organized by community supporters, like a yeshiva Purim banquet on Sunday, March 16, 1930 (Shushan Purim).[70] However, yeshiva fundraising also took its leadership much farther afield. Thus, Rabbi Kramer spoke on behalf of the yeshiva in the synagogue in Akron, Ohio in May 1930.[71] Another example is a fundraising trip to Detroit made by Rabbi Ruderman, accompanied by newly ordained Rabbi Zvi Stillman, cousin of a prominent Detroit rabbi, in September 1931.[72]

The difficulties under which the New Haven Yeshiva of Cleveland lived were exacerbated by Rabbi Levenberg's prolonged absence. This is apparent in a letter sent from Rabbi Kramer to Rabbi Levenberg during this period. Rabbi Kramer wrote Rabbi Levenberg that "the yeshiva is getting along with great difficulty [*be-kevedut meod*]" and that its financial situation was very bad. Rabbi Kramer specified in the letter that he had received no pay in three weeks, and that his son-in-law, Rabbi Ruderman, had not been paid for an even longer

---

66 The article was copied ibid., 184–190.
67 Document preserved in KFA.
68 Ever, *Rabbi J. H. Levenberg*, 191.
69 Ibid., 262.
70 JW, n.d. (1930), KFA.
71 "Sheftel Kramer, College Leader, Will Give Talk," *Akron Beacon Journal*, May 17, 1930. I am grateful to Rabbi Yaakov Neuberger for this clipping.
72 "Cleveland School Dean a Guest Here," *Detroit Jewish Chronicle*, October 2, 1931, 6, accessed December 5, 2021, https://digital.bentley.umich.edu/djnews/djc.1931.10.02.001/6.

period. Rabbi Kramer also complained that Rabbi Levenberg had not replied to several of his letters.[73]

From this letter, it also seems that Rabbi Levenberg was considering a trip to Cleveland for a rabbinical ordination celebration, an event calculated to present the New Haven Yeshiva to the public in a positive manner, counteract recent negative publicity, and aid fundraising. Seven New Haven Yeshiva graduates were ordained on March 8, 1931: Rabbis Zvi Stollman, Eliezer Meskin, Charles Batt (1904–1978),[74] Moshe Aryeh Kustanovitz (d. 1949), Mordecai Frimak, Mordecai S. Stovner, and Moshe A. Parzen. A special issue of the yeshiva bulletin was prepared; the ceremony was held in the presence of distinguished Rabbi Moshe Simon Sivitz of Pittsburgh (d. 1936).[75] The ordination diploma given to Rabbi Charles Batt on this occasion addressed itself directly to congregations who considered hiring these graduates by stating "The congregation that will accept him as its [spiritual] guide [moreh] will find in him all the things needed for a spiritual leader to be active in the affairs of the city."[76]

However, whatever boost the ordination ceremony gave the yeshiva, its situation remained critical. While the yeshiva's community board of directors tried by every means not to openly publicize this dire fact, according to a *Yiddishe Velt* article of May 22, 1932, the New Haven Yeshiva had taken a turn for the worse. Its deficit had increased; its building had been closed. The yeshiva's supporters announced a "dollar drive" with the goal of raising $5000.00 to ensure the yeshiva's existence through numerous individual contributions of one dollar. That same article contained important news that would constitute a potential game-changer for the yeshiva: Rabbi Levenberg, after an absence of some two-and-a-half years, was at last coming to settle in Cleveland.[77]

On August 19, 1932, Rabbi Levenberg returned to Cleveland, together with his wife and family.[78] He would not return as rabbi of Chibas Jerusalem as originally planned, however. He came instead to fill the role of the Cleveland Orthodox community's Chief Rabbi. As far as the New Haven Yeshiva was concerned, Rabbi Levenberg's return brought into the open a rift between him and Rabbis Kramer and Ruderman over who controlled the yeshiva. Rabbi Levenberg claimed precedence as the founder of the yeshiva; Rabbis Kramer

---

73 Ever, *Rabbi J. H. Levenberg*, 194–195.
74 "Rabbi Charles M. Batt," *New York Times*, June 20, 1978, Section B, 12.
75 Ever, *Rabbi J. H. Levenberg*, 196.
76 I am grateful to Rabbi Yaakov Neuberger for an image of this document.
77 JW, May 22, 1932.
78 Ever, *Rabbi J. H. Levenberg*, 203.

and Ruderman, who had been left to manage the precarious day-to-day existence of the yeshiva in Rabbi Levenberg's prolonged absence, had an entirely different perspective.

This contentious issue exploded in early 1933, and divided the yeshiva as well as the Jewish community, which had been already deeply divided on the issue of Rabbi Levenberg's communal leadership.[79] Yeshiva students discovered that they had to take sides, and those who favored Rabbi Levenberg experienced strained relations with the other *roshei yeshiva*. In the yeshiva, Rabbi Kramer allegedly called pro-Levenberg students derogatory names like "bums" and "Bolsheviks." Ever implies as well that Rabbi Kramer had a hand in anti-Levenberg propaganda with respect to kashrut disputes on the side of the opposition Cleveland kashrut organization, Misrad ha-Rabbonim.[80] Different factions of yeshiva students published open letters in successive issues of the *Yiddishe Velt*, March 13 and 17, 1933, as did different factions of community supporters of the yeshiva.[81] Communal meetings on the subject of the New Haven Yeshiva ended in blows.

Samuel Rocker published an editorial on the yeshiva issue in the *Yiddishe Velt* of March 22, 1933 in which he expressed his puzzlement: "The story of the yeshiva dispute is not yet sufficiently clarified, however one can more or less come to an approximate conclusion [*mesha'er*]." Rocker's conclusion was favorable to Rabbis Kramer and Ruderman. He asserted that Rabbi Levenberg had abandoned the yeshiva. Rocker stated: "What happened then is still not well-known. What is known is that Rabbi Kramer took over the yeshiva." Rocker continued by relating that afterwards Rabbi Kramer's son-in-law, Rabbi Ruderman, joined him. Under the leadership of these two great Torah scholars (*gedolei Torah*), the yeshiva at first functioned well. A number of new students came, and seven students received their rabbinical ordination. During this period, the yeshiva bought its own building for study and prayer, as well as a dormitory and dining facility. All this could be credited to Rabbis Kramer and Ruderman, to a number of community members, and to the members of the Women's Auxiliary, who helped, especially with the dormitory. Cleveland Jews were proud of the yeshiva and its *roshei yeshiva*. Then, just as suddenly as he left, Rabbi Levenberg returned to Cleveland, claiming to be the yeshiva's head, and supplanting Rabbi Kramer.[82]

---

79 See Sherman, *Orthodox Judaism*; Robinson, "A Link in the Great American Chain," 27–28.
80 Ever, *Rabbi J. H. Levenberg*, 321.
81 Ibid., 251.
82 Ibid., 257–258.

Rabbi Levenberg responded to Rocker's editorial in a letter to the editor by alleging that Rabbis Kramer and Ruderman were spreading "astonishing" rumors. Rabbi Levenberg stated that it was never his intention to dismiss the two *roshei yeshiva* and claimed no right to do so. He further stated that he never wanted to be the yeshiva's director (*menahel*) in place of Rabbi Kramer, though he admitted that some community members (*ba'alei batim*) wanted him to do so. He declared that he had taken no money from the yeshiva and had no intention of doing so in the future. He accused his opponents of circulating defamatory letters. He further stated:

> I came to Cleveland with the purest of intentions for the yeshiva and its directors. I have seen the yeshiva's terrible financial situation. I have seen the despair of many of the yeshiva students [*bnei yeshiva*]. I have a different vision of the yeshiva's future. . . . I want the yeshiva to grow, and be better and livelier.

Rabbi Levenberg decried what he characterized as a whispering campaign against him. He concluded that: "The yeshiva is worse now in all its aspects. I do not blame anyone, but this is not the yeshiva that is my ideal. I and the two *roshei yeshiva* should renew the yeshiva, which is now in danger."[83]

The dispute over control of the yeshiva was ultimately decided by the leadership of the Agudas ha-Rabbonim after Rabbis Kramer and Ruderman demanded a *din Torah* (rabbinical tribunal) against Rabbi Levenberg.[84] Rabbi Eliezer Silver (1882–1968) of Cincinnati, president of the Agudas ha-Rabbonim, took the lead in resolving the dispute and tried to formulate a compromise between the two sides, even though there was little possibility of peace, with each side completely contradicting its opponents' assertions.

The complex decision brokered by Rabbi Silver was published in full in the May 1933 issue of the Chicago-based rabbinical journal, *Ha-Pardes*, since it was evidently of high interest to the journal's rabbinical readers.[85] Rabbi Silver's compromise envisioned the direction of the yeshiva to be in the hands of all three disputing rabbis, with each of them possessing his own particular responsibilities. Rabbi Kramer would take care of the administrative direction of the yeshiva's affairs, such as calling meetings of the faculty and the community directors. Rabbi Ruderman would be in charge of teaching,

---

83 Ibid., 260–263.
84 Ibid., 255–256.
85 Eliezer Silver, "Yeshivas Nyu Haven be-Klivland," *Ha-Pardes* 7, no. 2 (May 1933): 27.

curriculum, and admissions. Rabbi Levenberg was to be the spiritual leader (*mashpi'a*) of the yeshiva. In cases of disputes between the rabbis, the compromise envisaged an arbitration (*baratungs*) committee consisting of five rabbis, two from Cleveland,[86] one from elsewhere in Ohio, and two designated by Agudas ha-Rabbonim.[87]

By July 11, 1933, this fragile compromise had broken down. At a meeting of a committee of the communal yeshiva supporters, who wanted an experienced accountant to examine the yeshiva financial records, Rabbis Kramer and Ruderman refused to hand over the records of the financial state of the institution. Rabbi Kramer argued that the rabbis, and no one else, were supposed to supervise the yeshiva's finances.[88] Rabbis Kramer and Ruderman were supported in their position in an editorial by Samuel Rocker in the *Yiddishe Velt*. Rocker contended that the communal directors had misinterpreted Rabbi Silver's decision.[89] Rabbis Kramer and Ruderman were also supported on this issue by the anti-Levenberg rabbinical coalition, Misrad ha-Rabbonim.[90] They prevailed in this round of the dispute as newly elected community directors backed down and expressed their desire to treat the incident as a misunderstanding.

At about this time, Rabbi Ruderman seized the opportunity to leave the New Haven Yeshiva for a post as rabbi in Baltimore. By August 23, 1933, he had left Cleveland along with some New Haven Yeshiva students, including those who came to the yeshiva from Baltimore, who would form the nucleus of the yeshiva he would found in that city.[91] Rabbi Ruderman's departure created an even more complex situation with respect to the New Haven Yeshiva's future. Some thought that with this state of affairs the yeshiva should give up on Cleveland altogether and go back to its original home in New Haven.[92] Now, Rabbi Kramer, facing Rabbi Levenberg by himself, moved to secure his own position. He asserted that the building at 880 Lakeview Road that housed the yeshiva did not in fact belong to the yeshiva. It had not been purchased directly for the yeshiva, but had rather been financed by a group of laymen

---

86 The document specifies that the two Cleveland rabbis were to come from Misrad ha-Rabbonim, the anti-Levenberg rabbinical coalition.
87 Ever, *Rabbi J. H. Levenberg*, 265–266.
88 Ibid., 321.
89 Ibid., 322.
90 Ibid., 323.
91 Ibid., 325.
92 Ibid., 327.

calling themselves the Ezras Torah Club, who intended it to be their synagogue with Rabbi Kramer as their rabbi.[93]

Such circumstances forced Rabbi Levenberg to respond. Because of his
extensive communal responsibilities as Chief Rabbi, he did not have time to
give the yeshiva his full attention. His contribution to the life of the yeshiva
since his return to Cleveland had been to present discourses on Sundays, and a
few classes during the week.[94] Clearly, he was unable to function as a full-time
rosh yeshiva, so he felt he needed to appoint a new *rosh yeshiva* to replace Rabbi
Ruderman, but Rabbi Kramer's continued presence made that course of action
very complicated, since according to Rabbi Silver's compromise, any important
decision for the yeshiva had to be taken with Rabbi Kramer's approval.

The threat of the appointment of a new *rosh yeshiva* spurred Samuel
Rocker, who had previously taken Rabbi Kramer's side on several disputed
issues, to publish a pro-Kramer editorial in the *Yiddishe Velt* of January 26, 1934.
The editorial called Rabbi Kramer a "great one in Israel [*gadol be-Yisrael*],"
and stated that Rabbi Kramer had headed the yeshiva with "respect, truth and
righteousness [*emes va-tsedek*]." Rabbi Kramer was a scholar (*talmid hakham*)
whose leadership all Cleveland should honor. The editorial warned Rabbi
Levenberg against replacing Rabbi Kramer. The editorial further supported
Rabbi Kramer's "ownership" of the yeshiva building and reported that since
Rabbi Ruderman had left for Baltimore, the New Haven Yeshiva had gone to
ruin and now had only fourteen students who were not studying Torah but
rather spending their time inciting against Rabbi Kramer.[95]

On January 28, 1934, this editorial was countered in a letter published in
the *Yiddishe Velt* by a group of eighteen pro-Levenberg students calling themselves the Students' Organization (*Histadrut ha-Talmidim*). The students
stated that they had been forced to proclaim the true situation of the yeshiva
since Rocker's editorial did not get its facts right. According to the students,
the yeshiva was now in a better situation than earlier. There were more than
fourteen students, and they were studying better than previously under Rabbi
Levenberg's influence. The students claimed that appointing a new *rosh yeshiva*
did not have as its purpose to dismiss Rabbi Kramer. On the other hand, the students continued, they needed a *rosh yeshiva* who would teach them, not Rabbi

93   Ibid., 327–328.
94   Ibid., 334.
95   Ibid., 329–330.

Kramer who was practicing dirty politics against the yeshiva and had organized a "club" that collected funds "for the yeshiva" under false pretenses.[96]

In the end, Rabbi Levenberg did manage to appoint a new *rosh yeshiva*, Rabbi Uri Meir Cirlin, who had studied in Europe with Rabbis Joseph Rosen (1858–1936) and Meir Simcha of Dvinsk (1843–1926), and who had been recommended by Rabbi Eliezer Silver.[97] This new *rosh yeshiva* arrived in Cleveland in January 1934.[98] In successfully appointing a new *rosh yeshiva*, Rabbi Levenberg had effectively seized control of the New Haven Yeshiva. From this point on, Rabbi Kramer does not appear as a factor in the affairs of the yeshiva, though his tombstone records his claim to be the "*rosh yeshiva* of Cleveland."[99]

A key symbol of Rabbi Levenberg successfully regaining control of the yeshiva he founded is the appearance of an issue of the yeshiva's student publication *Talmudist* on November 11, 1934, celebrating Rabbi Levenberg's fiftieth birthday, with Isaac Hirsch Ever as editor and Milton Dalin as co-editor.[100] This was the second and apparently last issue of the publication, and the only one known to be extant. A first issue does not survive, but apparently appeared in August 1933. It proclaimed itself a quarterly, appeared in magazine format, contained poetry as well as prose, and was reviewed in the *Tog*, the *Morgen Journal*, and the *Yiddishe Velt* in August 1933.[101]

Having regained his control over the yeshiva, Rabbi Levenberg maintained the threefold division of labor envisaged in Rabbi Silver's compromise. Rabbi Cirlin was now the *rosh yeshiva*; Rabbi Levenberg retained his role as "spiritual mentor" to the students. To oversee the administrative side of the yeshiva, formerly Rabbi Kramer's task, Rabbi Levenberg appointed a young graduate of the yeshiva, Rabbi Seymour (Zemach) Zambrowsky, as Registrar, a move that relieved Rabbi Levenberg of routine administrative responsibilities and ensured that the yeshiva administrator, as a junior appointee, would not exercise significant power within the yeshiva.

After the crisis, the yeshiva's finances seemed relatively stable, and announcements of yeshiva fundraising events did not contain the tone of

---

96 Ibid., 333–334.
97 On Rabbi Chirlin, see Yiddishe Velt farums, accessed December 4, 2021, https://www.ivelt. com/forum/viewtopic.php?t=11864&start=1050.
98 Ever, *Rabbi J. H. Levenberg*, 328–329.
99 Kevarim.com, accessed December 2, 2021, http://kevarim.com/rabbi-sheftel-kramer/.
100 Ever, *Der Talmudist*; Cf. Ever, *Rabbi J. H. Levenberg*, 341.
101 Ever, *Rabbi J. H. Levenberg*, 326.

desperation of those from May 1932. Examples of community fundraising initiatives in 1934 include a post-Shabbat (*melava malka*) celebration accompanied by a raffle, for which the grand prize was a refrigerator valued at $150.00.[102] Another example of yeshiva community-oriented programming is a Friday night Hanukah celebration at the yeshiva, with speakers including Rabbis Levenberg and Cirlin, as well as Rabbi Leon Elkind, supervisor of Cleveland's Orthodox Jewish Orphanage, and Isaac Hirsch Ever, speaking on behalf of the students' organization. That program was chaired by the yeshiva's Registrar Rabbi Zambrowsky, while Abraham Aronovitz led the yeshiva students in a musical program.[103]

Other community fundraising and programming initiatives from this period include a Yeshiva Sisterhood-sponsored bazaar held on Saturday night, January 13, 1934, with proceeds in support of the yeshiva.[104] From that same period comes an article printed in the *Yiddishe Velt* in which the yeshiva publicly thanked a number of businesses and individuals who contributed goods or services to the yeshiva, indicating that there were means of supporting the yeshiva and its students other than the raising of money.

- Kenmore Dairy Company donated a weekly gallon of cream.
- Heights Baking Company donated bread for three weeks.
- Echo Dairy Company donated thirty-six bottles of milk daily.[105]
- Bruder Creamery Stores donated every week milk, butter, cheese, and cream.
- Weiss Baking Company donated bread every week.
- Three butchers were thanked for giving twenty-five pounds of meat each.
- Two men were thanked for painting the yeshiva's study lecterns (*shtenders*).
- Several doctors were thanked for treating yeshiva students gratis.
- L. Manheim was thanked for donating for thirty-five pounds of fish and two chickens.[106]

Beyond local fundraising, the yeshiva continued to ask for donations in other North American cities. An example is a fundraising trip to Detroit

---

102 JW, November 6, 1934.
103 JW, December 7, 1934, 2; JW, November 23, 1934, 7.
104 JW, undated clipping, KFA.
105 Thirty-six bottles of milk daily may be an approximate indication of the number of yeshiva students at this time.
106 JW, undated clipping, KFA.

undertaken on July 26, 1935, in which Rabbi Milton (Elimelech) Dalin, then the yeshiva's Registrar,[107] evidently having succeeded Rabbi Zambrowsky in that position, led the delegation.[108]

However, Rabbi Levenberg had evidently also begun thinking of gathering funds for the yeshiva on a national scale. Thus on January 22, 1935, a letter was sent on yeshiva letterhead to a Mr. Sobol, informing him that, at a meeting of the board and faculty of the yeshiva, he had been appointed an honorary member of the institution's National Board of Directors. Sobol was urged to support a yeshiva that had been "acclaimed" by the Agudas ha-Rabbonim, Rabbi Abraham Isaac Kook, Chief Rabbi of British-Mandate Palestine, and "European Roshei Yeshiva." Supporting yeshiva students from all over the country as well as many foreign students, the New Haven Yeshiva was preparing a Jewish leadership "to meet the needs of today."[109] Similarly, Isaac Hirsch Ever, quoted in an article in the New York's *Tog* of April 28, 1935, asserted that the scope of the New Haven Yeshiva was not local, but national. Finally, in December 1935, Rabbi Levenberg travelled to Detroit for a speech opening a $50,000 campaign on behalf of the New Haven Yeshiva in order "to realize [its] planned expansion program."[110]

Once Rabbi Cirlin had been accepted as *rosh yeshiva* by the yeshiva students, new students began to arrive at the yeshiva.[111] The most publicized of these students was a fifteen-year-old boy from New York, Abraham Orbach, who had been a student at the Tifereth Jerusalem Yeshiva in New York, and had determined to run away from home to enroll in the New Haven Yeshiva, borrowing the $10.00 bus fare from New York to Cleveland for that purpose. Orbach's father, who opposed his son's intention, called on the Cleveland Police to arrest his son as a runaway. The police duly arrested Orbach, but required the father to come to Cleveland to pick up his son. When the father

---

107 Rabbi Milton Dalin went on to serve congregations in Iowa City, Cleveland and Wheeling, West Virginia. See "Judith Dalin Lee Elkind," Legacy.com, accessed December 1, 2021, https://www.legacy.com/obituaries/postgazette/obituary.aspx?n=judith-dalin-lee-elkind&pid=2447401&fhid=4365.

108 "Clevelanders Ask Fund for Seminary," *Detroit Jewish Chronicle*, July 26, 1935, 8, accessed December 1, 2021, https://digital.bentley.umich.edu/djnews/djc.1935.07.26.001/8.

109 Seymour M. (Zemach) Zambrowsky, Registrar of the New Haven Yeshiva to [no first name given] Sobol, January 22, 1935, KFA.

110 "Rabbi Levenberg will Speak Here," *Detroit Jewish Chronicle*, December 20, 1935, 2, accessed December 5, 2021, https://digital.bentley.umich.edu/djnews/djc.1935.12.20.001/2.

111 Ever, *Rabbi J. H. Levenberg*, 334.

was unable or unwilling to do so, the boy was allowed to remain in the New Haven Yeshiva.[112]

However, Rabbi Cirlin's tenure at the New Haven Yeshiva was comparatively brief. He left Cleveland and took a post in Los Angeles, California because its climate was more conducive to his health. This left Rabbi Levenberg with the urgent task of appointing a new *rosh yeshiva*, for, without a *rosh yeshiva*, students began to leave. At meetings held in January and February 1937, the yeshiva made the decision to appoint a new *rosh yeshiva* as well as a new office manager.[113] Ultimately, two new *roshei yeshiva* were appointed: Rabbi Moshe Feinstein (1895–1986), newly arrived in the United States from Liuban, Russia, and Rabbi Chaim Moshe Reuven Elazary (1902–1984), identified as having come to America from Palestine.[114] Based on these new hires, the yeshiva mounted a renewed effort to fundraise through appeals in Cleveland congregations on Passover.[115] Rabbis Feinstein and Elazary were welcomed to Cleveland at an inaugural banquet held at Chibas Jerusalem on April 11, 1937 attended by some 500 people.[116] Speaking at the banquet were several Cleveland rabbis as well as other prominent speakers,[117] including Rabbi Reuben Levovitz (d. 1965) of New York, brother-in-law of Rabbi Feinstein. In April 1937 as well, in an attempt to broaden the yeshiva's student base, the New Haven Yeshiva, for the first time, announced that it would accept young boys as students.[118] However, this would be the yeshiva's last attempt at innovation to improve its fortunes.

In the first half of 1937, the yeshiva's community support system seems to have functioned relatively normally. An indication of this is the series of

---

112 "East Side Irate as Father Has Would-be Rabbi Son Arrested," *Jewish Telegraphic Agency Daily Bulletin*, December 28, 1934, https://www.jta.org/archive/east-side-irate-as-father-has-would-be-rabbi-son-arrested, accessed December 4, 2021; "Youth to be Rabbi despite Father," American Jewish World, January 11, 1935, 1–2, accessed December 4, 2021. https://www.nli.org.il/en/newspapers/?a=is&oid=amjwld19350111-01.2.3&type=nlilogi calsectionpdf&e=-------en-20--1--img-txIN%7ctxTI-------------1.

113 JW, January 19 and February 5, 1937; WPA 1937, 277.

114 JW, March 23, 1937; WPA 1937, 277. One source states that Rabbi Elazary was the rabbi of Congregation Agudas Achim in Canton, Ohio from 1929. However, if this were so, the Cleveland newspaper would not omit that fact. After the NHYC ended, he did become rabbi in Canton, Ohio. See "Todays' Yahrzeits in History, 7–8 Iyar," Matzav.com (link inactive now), accessed December 2, 2021, https://matzav.com/todays-yahrzeits-history-7-8-iyar/.

115 JW, March 26, 1937; WPA 1937, 277.

116 JW, April 1, 1937; WPA 1937, 171; JW, April 13, 1937; WPA 1937, 311.

117 JW, April 7, 1937; WPA 1937, 277.

118 JW, April 16, 1937; WPA 1937, 277.

reports of numerous Yeshiva Sisterhood activities in 1937 published in the *Yiddishe Velt* from January to early June.

- January 1: Mrs. F. Wax, president, announces that a meeting will be held . . . tomorrow. An arrangement committee for the jubilee will be appointed.
- January 8: Mrs. Birnbaum, publicity secretary, announces that at the election of officers January 6 the following were chosen: Mesdames Garber, Kramer, and Gudin, presidents; Mesdames Semter, Burstein, and Leventhal, vice presidents; Mrs. Sarah Siegel, treasurer; and Mrs. Berman, recording secretary.
- January 8: A *M'Lave Malke* (End of the Sabbath) celebration will be held at the Seminary tomorrow night. This affair is to be in honor of the newly elected officers. A musical program will be presented.
- January 19: It was decided that a luncheon should be held . . . tomorrow. Mrs. Siegel will be chairman and Mrs. Berman co-chairman. An interesting program has been prepared.
- January 31: On January 27 a Fifteenth day of the month of Shvat party was held. A. Lifshitz, who was toastmaster, introduced the following speakers: Berenzweig, President of the Seminary, Gudin, and Mrs. Kramer. Rabbi Yehuda Heshel Halevy Levenberg explained the meaning of the Fifteenth day of the month of Shvat. Thanks is given to Mrs. Lifshitz for her good work.
- January 31: The welfare of the Seminary will be discussed at a meeting Feb. 1 . . .
- February 12: For tomorrow night the sisterhood has arranged an End of the Sabbath feast in honor of the engagement of Rabbi Moses, a student of the Seminary, to the daughter of Teitelman of Thornhill Dr.
- February 18: Mrs. Ana Garber made an appeal for money at the Pidyon Haben (Redemption of the First Born Son) celebration of Sanford Garber at 10213 Parkgate Ave., and collected $10 for the Seminary.
- February 19: A Purim (Deliverance from Haman) party will be held tomorrow night. An oratorical and musical program will be presented.
- March 2: Mrs. Burstein is in charge of the luncheon to be held . . . today.
- April 7: At the meeting of March 30 it was decided to hold a luncheon . . . today. Mrs. H. Kramer, president, with Mesdames Seigel,

Garber, and Osman, promise an entertaining program. R. Burstein will be chairman.

- May 7: At a meeting tomorrow night arrangements will be made for the picnic. Mrs. Mesh, president, urges all members to attend.
- May 11: A luncheon will be held ... tomorrow. Mrs. Silver is chairman of the affair. Mesdames Garber, Semter, and Klima are among the hostesses. Final arrangements for the picnic were made. Committees were appointed to contact the Cleveland Jews for donations for the picnic. Mr. and Mrs. Leventhal are the chairmen of the picnic; Mr. and Mrs. Greenberg are the co-chairmen.
- June 4: The annual picnic will be held with the co-operation of the men's group, at Wade Park June 6. It is expected that this will be one of the most successful picnics. Everyone worked energetically and much merchandise was donated. Besides spending a full day of fun, the attendants will at the same time help with the noble work of the institution.[119]

Thus, fully fourteen Sisterhood programs are reported from January to June, 1937, including one devoted at least in part to planning for the fifteenth anniversary of the founding of the New Haven Yeshiva the next year, 1938. There is absolutely nothing published in the *Yiddishe Velt* on the Yeshiva Sisterhood after June, which indicates that the organization had stopped its programming, likely because after June the New Haven Yeshiva was on its last legs. Rabbi Levenberg was ill, and new students were not appearing.[120] The feeling of decline in the yeshiva is revealed in a letter Rabbi Feinstein wrote from Cleveland to Rabbi Israel Rosenberg (1875–1956) in New York on 22 Sivan 5697 [June 1, 1937]:

> I know that you, my friend, want to see me in a situation that is proper and lasting. To my regret, I am unable to tell you that this is so, for because of our many sins I have not yet found rest, and it does not appear that there is a future here that is suitable for me according to the situation I found.[121]

Tellingly, when Rabbi Feinstein moved to Cleveland in April 1937, he left his family in New York.

---

119 WPA 1937, 277–279.
120 Ever, *Rabbi J. H. Levenberg*, 345.
121 Moshe Feinstein, *Igrot Moshe*, vol. 8 (New York, 1997), 24.

By November 1937, with Rabbi Levenberg in failing health, it had become apparent that the New Haven Yeshiva of Cleveland had no future. The last question dealt with seems to have been the disposal of the yeshiva's premises. In November 1937, the yeshiva leadership met with Cleveland's Young Israel Congregation, and the yeshiva building was sold to Young Israel.[122] In December 1937, the *Yiddishe Velt* reported that Rabbi Levenberg was leaving Cleveland because of ill health.[123] He would die in New York the next month.[124] In the *Yiddishe Velt* reportage of Rabbi Levenberg's funeral, the New Haven Yeshiva is referred to as "former," and in Rabbi Bick's 1939 article, the yeshiva is mentioned as having ceased with Rabbi Levenberg's death.[125]

V. A Failed Experiment?

Clearly, the New Haven Yeshiva failed to achieve the ambitions its founder had for it: to become a well-established Mussar yeshiva, attracting young Jewish men from throughout North America. However, did the yeshiva's short lifespan mean that it was a failed experiment? Certainly, the New Haven Yeshiva was an institution ahead of its time. It was founded in the 1920s, an era in which yeshiva education was almost entirely associated with Eastern Europe. It operated in a country in which even Orthodox Jews did not always see the value of advanced Talmudic learning. Furthermore, it existed outside the major centers of whatever yeshiva education existed in that period, New York and Chicago. Nonetheless, the New Haven Yeshiva did attract dozens of young American Jews to study Talmud in an institution modeled on the Slobodka Yeshiva, and granted a number of rabbinical ordinations. As well, the New Haven Yeshiva attracted a significant level of community support in both New Haven and Cleveland that would become an important factor for the future development of advanced yeshivot in North America.

The failure of the New Haven Yeshiva to endure largely stemmed from two factors. Perhaps the most important was the absence of its founder, Rabbi Levenberg, during the crucial two-year period of its transition from New Haven to Cleveland. This absence caused significant conflict in the yeshiva leadership that affected its ability to function effectively. The second factor was

---

122 JW, November 9 and 14, 1937; WPA 1937, 277–278.
123 JW, December 24, 1937; WPA 1937, 139.
124 JW, January 17–18, 1938; JW, March 18, 1938; WPA 1938, 148.
125 Bick, "A Koventsion," 9.

the worldwide economic depression that began at just the time the yeshiva transitioned from New Haven to Cleveland, which significantly hampered the yeshiva's ability to raise the funds it needed to function properly.

Cleveland Jewry lost the New Haven Yeshiva in 1937, but the community would not be without a yeshiva for long. In 1941, refugee Rabbis Eliyahu Meir Bloch (1895–1954) and Chaim Mordechai Katz (1894–1964) decided to locate their Telshe Yeshiva in Cleveland, with highly important consequences for the development of Cleveland's Orthodox community.[126] They had considered locating their institution in other Midwestern cities, such as Cincinnati, Pittsburgh and Detroit.[127] Why did they ultimately choose Cleveland? One important factor was likely that the New Haven Yeshiva had coalesced a relatively large and active group of Cleveland community supporters, men and women alike, who were receptive to the idea of supporting an institution of advanced rabbinical study in their community. Rabbi Bloch is reported to have said, "The old fire [of Torah] lit by Reb Yehuda Heschel [Levenberg] had not been extinguished."[128] The New Haven Yeshiva, therefore, did not simply disappear without trace. It had left a legacy among Cleveland Jews that undoubtedly aided the initial steps of the Telshe Yeshiva, which was established at a time that was, because of numerous factors, more receptive to the establishment of a yeshiva on North American soil.

---

126 "Telshe Yeshiva," ECH, accessed December 1, 2021, https://case.edu/ech/articles/t/ telshe-yeshiva.
127 See chapter two in this volume.
128 Zivitofsky, "Torah Shines Forth," 22.

CHAPTER 6

"The Second Destruction of Cleveland Orthodox Synagogues": Rabbi Israel Porath and Cleveland Jewry at the Crossroads, 1945

Introduction

In late March 1945, as World War II in Europe was nearing its end, an Orthodox rabbi in Cleveland, Ohio wrote an article for the local Yiddish newspaper, the *Yiddishe Velt* (Jewish World) that encompassed a remarkably clear analysis of the situation of Cleveland's Orthodox Jewry at that time[1] and a prescient vision of its suburban future.[2]

---

1   On the situation of North American Orthodox Jewry in the immediate postwar period, see Zev Eleff, "From Teacher to Scholar to Pastor: The Evolving Postwar Modern Orthodox Rabbinate," *American Jewish History* 98 (October 2014): 289–313; Lawrence Grossman, "American Orthodoxy in the 1950s: The Lean Years," in *Rav Chesed: Essays in Honor of Rabbi Dr. Haskel Lookstein* (Hoboken, NJ: KTAV, 2009), 251–269; Haym Soloveitchik, "Rupture and Reconstruction: The Transformation of Contemporary Orthodoxy," *Tradition* 28 (Summer 1994): 64–130. More generally, see Jeffrey Gurock, *From Fluidity to Rigidity: The Religious Worlds of Conservative and Orthodox Jews in Twentieth-Century America* (Ann Arbor: Jean and Samuel Frankel Center for Judaic Studies, the University of Michigan, 1998); Zev Eleff, ed., *Modern Orthodox Judaism: A Documentary History* (Philadelphia: Jewish Publication Society, 2016).

2   For a discussion of North American postwar suburbanization, see Doug Owram, *Born at the Right Time: A History of the Baby-Boom Generation* (Toronto: University of Toronto

The rabbi's name was Israel Porath (1886–1974).[3] Born in Jerusalem, Rabbi Porath, who was a student of Rabbi Abraham Isaac Kook, came to the United States in 1923 and served at first as rabbi in Plainfield, New Jersey. In 1925, he came to Cleveland, having been offered a rabbinical position by Cleveland's Congregation Ohab Zedek.[4] Beyond his considerable erudition, Rabbi Porath brought to Cleveland an ability to articulate his ideas in nearly flawless English.[5] By 1927, Rabbi Porath was taking a leading role in Cleveland's orthodox rabbinate,[6] aiming to solve the contentious issues related to the city's kosher meat industry.[7] Cleveland's kashrut was an issue that, as he stated, "embittered our communal life for decades and that constantly brought with it so much desecration [*hillul ha-shem*] and distress [*agmat nefesh*] that it seemed that kosher meat and conflict were like Siamese twins that cannot be separated."[8] It would not be until 1940 that a new rabbinic organization under Rabbi Porath's leadership, the Orthodox Rabbinical Council (Merkaz ha-Rabbonim), managed to achieve the unity that had eluded Cleveland Orthodoxy until then and was able, in cooperation with Cleveland's Jewish Federation, to create a stable kashrut supervision in Cleveland that lasted for decades.[9]

Rabbi Porath devoted his scholarly work to the writing and publication of *Mavo ha-Talmud* (seven volumes), a guide making Talmud study easier both for young students who had never studied Gemara and for adults who had studied in their youth but had forgotten their learning.[10]

Press, 1996), chapter 3; Dolores Hayden, *Building Suburbia: Green Fields and Urban Growth, 1820–2000* (New York: Pantheon Books, 2003). On the suburbanization of Orthodox Jews, see Etan Diamond, *And I Will Dwell in their Midst: Orthodox Jews in Suburbia* (Chapel Hill: University of North Carolina Press, 2000); idem, "The Kosher Lifestyle: Religious Consumerism and Suburban Orthodox Jews," *Journal of Urban History* 28, no. 4 (2002): 488–505; Albert I. Gordon, *Jews in Suburbia* (Boston: Beacon Press, 1959), 85–127.

3 On Rabbi Porath, see Israel Porath, *Mishkaotekha Yisrael* (Jerusalem: Porath, 2017), introduction. For a wealth of documentary material on Rabbi Porath, see "Rabbi Israel Porath, 1886–1974." The major account of the history of the Cleveland Jewish community to the mid-twentieth century remains Gartner, *History of the Jews of Cleveland*. On Cleveland's Orthodox community, see chapters one and two in this volume.

4 Wertheim and Bennett, *Remembering: Cleveland's Jewish Voices*, 203.

5 Many of Porath's English-language sermons, including his inaugural sermon from 1925 are preserved in the Rabbi Israel Porath Papers WRHS MSS 4753, container 2, folder 7.

6 "Visiting Orthodox Rabbis of Three States Welcomed Here."

7 In AJYB 29 (1927–1928): 210, a group called "The Orthodox United Rabbinate of Cleveland" claimed to have eight members with Porath as chairman.

8 "Vi azoi hot der merkaz ha-rabbonim bahandelt di kashrus frage letstn yor?"

9 Vincent and Rubenstein, *Merging Traditions*, 57.

10 Porath, *Mavo ha-Talmud*, vol. 1: *Gittin*, introduction. It is noteworthy that Cleveland Reform Rabbi Abba Hillel Silver donated $500.00 toward the publication of one of Rabbi

In the 1940s, the Cleveland Jewish community stood at a crossroads.[11] When Rabbi Porath had arrived in Cleveland in the 1920s, the center of the Eastern European immigrant community and its synagogues had been the "Central" neighborhood,[12] and Rabbi Porath had witnessed the influx of African-Americans and the exodus of Jews from that neighborhood. Cleveland Jews then moved to two new neighborhoods: one, Glenville, coalesced around East 105th Street; the other encompassed the Kinsman Road district. By 1945, however, Cleveland Jewry found itself under pressure to move once again.

As his article shows, Rabbi Porath saw the Cleveland Jewish situation both as a crisis and as an opportunity. He felt that there was an urgent need for Cleveland's Orthodox Jewry to take stock of itself in this transitional period. In particular, Rabbi Porath urged synagogue leaders not to repeat their previous mistake of rebuilding existing synagogues separately in new neighborhoods. Synagogues should rather try to combine forces and establish an Orthodox bloc to influence the Jewish Community Council. And indeed, in the spirit of Rabbi Porath's vision, the Jewish Community Council and Federation did meet with the Orthodox synagogues to help them plan their eventual move to the Heights area.[13] Influence was exerted to effect synagogue mergers so as to establish large conglomerate Orthodox congregations, like the Taylor Road Synagogue, the Heights Jewish Center, and the Warrensville Center Synagogue with a higher membership base. Thus, for example, the Warrensville Center Synagogue, dedicated in April, 1959, encompassed three congregations from the previous area: the Tetiever Ahavas Achim Anshe Sfard, Bnai Jacob Kol Israel (Kinsman Jewish Center), and Neve Zedek with a combined membership of over 1,000 families.[14] As Rabbi Porath stated at the new synagogue's dedication:

> The shifting of population from the city to the suburbs has changed the whole structure of our local Orthodox Jewry. Old and long-established congregations, which had existed for many

---

Porath's books. Abba Hillel Silver to Israel Porath, November 17, 1954, Israel Porath Papers, WRHS 1, folder 2.

11 For an account of the similar developments in the Jewish community of Detroit in this era, see Lila Corwin Berman, *Metropolitan Jews: Politics, Race, and Religion in Postwar Detroit* (Chicago: University of Chicago Press, 2015).

12 "Central Neighborhood," ECH, accessed March 7, 2018, https://case.edu/ech/articles/c/central-neighborhood/.

13 Vincent, *Personal and Professional*, 180. On the development of suburb of Cleveland Heights, see Marian Morton, "The Suburban Ideal and Suburban Realities: Cleveland Heights, Ohio, 1860–2001," *Journal of Urban History* 28, no. 6 (2002): 671–698.

14 "Three Cleveland Orthodox Congregations Announce Merger."

scores of years in the old neighborhoods, had to be reshaped through mergers.[15]

As a result of this planning process, Taylor Road in Cleveland Heights became in the 1950s a street central to the Orthodox community, which included the Hebrew Academy day school, several synagogues, kosher bakeries, and food stores.[16]

The Article: Der Tzveyter Hurbn fun Klivlander Orthodoksishe Shuln (The Second Destruction of Cleveland Orthodox Synagogues)[17]

by Rabbi Israel Porath

Twenty-five years ago in Cleveland there was a flourishing Jewish settlement on Cedar and Central Avenues and their vicinity. There existed large, magnificent synagogues with beautiful study houses, which were packed with Jews who prayed in several *minyanim*[18] each day and which housed tables and benches where Torah scholars and those who had acquired [Torah] learning would study daily portions of Talmud, Mishna, *Eyn Ya'akov*,[19] etc. These were Jews from the old country and synagogues in the old style.

After a while there came prosperity and the Jews began to run from their homes. In a short time the entire Jewish settlement there was destroyed. Many synagogues were sold as churches; the rest were left empty and abandoned and a significant Jewish resource was lost.

In those years the banks gave mortgages for community buildings. The [congregations] bought and built large new synagogues in the two new Jewish settlements around 105th Street and around Kinsman Road. In these synagogues the study sessions were smaller and fewer, but people still prayed. Many synagogues had three *minyanim* and others two, but it became a more compact Jewish community.

---

15 Rabbi Israel Porath Papers MSS 4753, WRHS, folder 8.
16 Vincent and Rubenstein, *Merging Traditions*, 20.
17 JW, March 28, 1945, 2. Translated from the Yiddish by Ira Robinson.
18 In this context, *minyan* means a Jewish prayer service.
19 A compendium of the non-halakhic content of the Talmud, edited in the sixteenth century by Rabbi Jacob ibn Habib.

The community built a community *mikveh*[20] with modern and hygienic fixtures, which cost tens of thousands of dollars. There were also magnificent institutions like the Old Age Home,[21] the Orphanage,[22] and later the Hakhnosos Orkhim.[23] As well, the Yeshiva Adas [Bnei Yisroel][24] and the Talmud Torahs placed their central institutions and their branches in the new Jewish neighborhood and a great Jewish community was formed anew that pulsated with life and activity. A traditional Jewish community was established with the old attributes.

As was mentioned, all the synagogues were mortgaged by the banks. However, five years ago, there began a movement to pay off the mortgages. The Neve Zedek Shul was the first to publicize its joy at burning the mortgage and, soon after, other synagogues were freed from debt and became a Jewish community possession in the full sense of the term.

After a while there was once again a tumult. Jews began to flee from their beautiful middle-class homes. At the beginning this flight was sporadic and intermittent, later it was at a quicker pace and in masses. The prosperity coming from the bloody war has once more made everyone drunk. We see once again how Jewish neighborhoods are becoming abandoned and emptied. It is now a normal experience to see great Houses of Study looking for a tenth man for a *minyan*. If this goes on we will once more see the old spectacle that we now experience regarding the old Jewish neighborhoods. Parents will travel downtown with their children and show them the churches where Sammy became bar mitzvah, where Eddy graduated, and where Charlie and Penny were married.

Yes, this appears to be the situation. The synagogues that have just been freed from their mortgages are simultaneously becoming abandoned by their members and supporters. The Conservative element has more or less adjusted to the new surroundings and has already been consolidated with local schools and activities. However, the Orthodox element, which always sees itself as coming too little too late, goes about in the new areas like wandering sheep. There has suddenly come a crisis in their long-established way of life and they feel that they have somehow lost their footing.

---

20 Ritual pool.
21 Founded in 1906, and in 1945 situated on Lakeview Avenue.
22 Chartered in May, 1919 and opened in August, 1920 as the Orthodox Jewish Orphan Asylum.
23 A traditional institution giving shelter to itinerant Jews.
24 Founded in 1915. Gartner, *History of the Jews of Cleveland*, 287.

I want to point out that this misfortune would not be so great if our communal life was not so concentrated around the synagogues. In a city with a *Kultus-Gemeinde*,[25] when [Jews] move from one neighborhood to another, [the *Kultus-Gemeinde*] takes with it all the communal institutions, which will continue functioning on the same basis as previously. In the Land of Israel or in Diaspora countries from which the local Jewish population came, synagogues constitute a part of the general communal property, like the Talmud Torah, kosher meat, old age home, orphanage, *mikveh*, etc. However, in American Jewish life, synagogues function as separate communities. Each synagogue constitutes an institution by itself, with its own membership and functions. There is a mutual influence and feeling of loyalty between the synagogue and its members, the sisterhoods and men's clubs and with the children's schools. Each synagogue justifies its own existence according to its own vision and ability. And when a sudden crisis erupts it is brought to a serious state of affairs.

Simultaneously with the decline of the synagogues, the Orthodox Jewry of Cleveland has also experienced in the past three years great losses. The entire traditional way of life has been shattered. The hygienic *mikveh* that was purchased with communal money has become the private property of individuals. These individuals have found that from a financial standpoint they can do without continuing the hygienic regime of cleanliness and exactness. As soon as it becomes a private business, no one else's opinion counts and no one can demand that they go to the extra expense.

Three years ago there existed a rabbinic supervision over kosher meat that was satisfactory and effective. Lately the question of supervision of kashrut has completely disappeared from current concern. Today there is no supervision at all, neither over kosher meat nor delicatessen. As well, the supervision in the slaughterhouses has become significantly weakened. A slaughterhouse that once had four rabbinical supervisors has, bit by bit, gotten rid of three and the one who remains is on sufferance.

The foundation of traditional Jewish family life has begun to crack and the entire edifice is teetering. Jewish divorces according to the Law of Moses and Israel have been reduced to a minimum. This is already an old trouble. However, now we are also threatened by a wave of mixed marriages. This plague, which until not long ago was felt only in the smaller cities in which

---

25 A citywide Jewish communal organization that took care of all the needs of the Jewish community. This sort of community organization characterized European Jewry but not American Jewry.

only a few Jewish families lived, has begun to appear and spread also in larger communities, and Cleveland has found itself strongly affected by the assault. This is a growing phenomenon in which the Conservative element needs to be interested as well.

Among our defeats we need to consider that of our local newspaper, the *Jewish World*, which has had to stop publication as a daily paper. It is only thanks to the devotion of the employees that is was possible to continue its publication as a weekly.[26]

***

It is self-evident that the abovementioned problems are not just Cleveland problems. All of them are shared by many. In all cities there are Jewish neighborhoods that are decaying. Family purity is a vexed issue that we do not speak of. Kosher meat is an old, talked-out issue. Mixed marriages have become a nationwide disease. Yiddish newspapers in Philadelphia and Chicago have gone under.

Certainly, Cleveland is but a link in the great American chain. However, that does not mean that we can ignore our local problems because other Jewish communities suffer from the same troubles. When there is an outbreak of plague, each locality must undertake its own measures to protect and save itself from destruction.

I think that now, when Cleveland's Orthodox Jewry is packing to move to a new neighborhood, is the right time to evaluate our circumstances and weakness. Now is the right time for many in the remaining remnant of synagogues to not make the same mistake of moving all existing synagogues but on a smaller scale. A way must be found that several synagogues can combine forces so that it will be possible to found two or three larger synagogues in different parts of the Heights. (I do not want to advise that we should contemplate a synagogue that is too large and powerful because the experience of the [Cleveland] Jewish Center demonstrated that Orthodoxy is not strong enough to protect its interests in time of crisis. There must remain some reserves to protect the

---

26 *Jewish World* (*Yiddishe Velt*) was founded in 1907 and ceased publication in 1952. "Cleveland Yiddish Newspaper Ceases Publication, Existed since 1907," JTA, March 6, 1952, accessed March 7, 2018, https://www.jta.org/1952/03/06/archive/cleveland-yiddish-newspaper-ceases-publication-existed-since-1907.

balance between the aspirations for modernity and the nostalgia for authentic tradition).[27]

The coming together of the new settlement in the Heights is in certain respects different from the settlement that happened twenty-five years ago. Then the different elements could be divided into three. The neighborhood between Superior and St. Clair was mostly settled by businessmen and the middle class. The Kinsman neighborhood was taken by the working classes and the Heights was occupied by the professional classes. Now the new settlement will be made up of all three classes together: professionals, businessmen and workers. This fact will certainly have an influence on the establishment of the religious and cultural life of the area. I think that now is the best time for the presidents and directors of the Lithuanian, Polish, Galician, Grodner, Tetiever Synagogues, etc., to come together to discuss the problem and decide to adopt measures for a united plan on how to save the synagogues from total disappearance. There are a few synagogues here that deal now only with a cemetery, and a number of others are destined for the same fate.

The time has also come that Orthodox elements must group together in a strong block in the [Jewish] Community Council. This council is a democratic institution that has existed for a good number of years. Nearly all the synagogues are represented, however, until now they have not shown their strength. A strong block with a rational plan and policies would have a great influence on the entire thought process of the council. For example, it would not be any sin to exert pressure through the council on the Welfare Federation, which makes a campaign for over one million dollars a year that it should allocate a few thousand dollars to make order in the kashrut question in order to be rid of the constant scandals and desecrations, which were only caused by monetary issues. It is my impression that now is the optimum time for a satisfactory solution to these incessant problems to be made without substantial opposition. The overwhelming majority of the local rabbis is ready to cooperate in such an undertaking. There must, however, be a legal and well-appointed committee that will understand how to handle the problem in a practical manner.

The proper organization that could give itself to the solution of all the above mentioned and similar problems should be the Mizrachi Council of Cleveland. To the council belong many synagogues that understand more

---

27 On the conflictual conversion of the Cleveland Jewish Center from Orthodoxy to Conservatism in the 1920s, see chapter four in this volume.

or less the importance of organization in community life. The council must not limit its influence only to gather money for the Mizrachi [movement]. It must deepen and enlarge its activities in the area of strengthening the Torah and Judaism, especially in the area of Jewish education, on a purely traditional basis.

For this purpose it would be necessary to utilize our old-new weekly the *Jewish World* to illuminate all these questions and to shape public opinion that should not be focused on scathing criticism and strife, but only on earnest constructive work to be done with reason and persistence.

And if not now, when?[28]

---

28 M Avot 1:14.

Index

Ingram Content Group UK Ltd.
Milton Keynes UK
UKHW052328290523
422459UK00025B/179